Ages 5-10

Reproducible!

The SUPER-SIZED

Book of Holidays, Special Days, & Celebrations

Bible Activities for the Whole Year

ROSEKiDZ

The Super-Sized Book of Holidays, Special Days, and Celebrations
© 2021 Rose Publishing, LLC

Published by RoseKidz®
An imprint of Hendrickson Publishing Group
Rose Publishing, LLC
P.O. Box 3473
Peabody, Massachusetts 01961-3473 USA
www.hendricksonpublishinggroup.com

All rights reserved.

Managing Editor: Karen McGraw
Editorial and Production Associate: Drew McCall
Assistant Editor: Talia Messina
Cover Design: Drew McCall

Conditions of Use
Permission is granted* to make up to 300 copies of individual pages** from this book for classroom use only. The pages may not be modified in any manner. Permission is not granted to modify pages, to reprint charts, maps, time lines, and images apart from the page setting, to reprint groups of pages in bound form, either electronically or physically, or to offer copies for sale or donation either at cost or profit. All commercial use of this material is reserved by Rose Publishing, LLC. These pages, charts, maps, time lines, and images may not be placed nor used on websites. Any other use must be approved in writing by Rose Publishing, LLC.

*Do not make any copies from this book unless you adhere strictly to the guidelines found on this page.
**Pages with the following notation can be legally reproduced:

© 2021 Rose Publishing, LLC. Permission to photocopy granted to original purchaser only. The Super-Sized Book of Holidays, Special Days, Celebrations.

All Scripture quotations are taken from the Holy Bible, New Living Translation, copyright © 1996, 2004, 2015 by Tyndale House Foundation. Used by permission of Tyndale House Publishers, Inc., Carol Stream, Illinois 60188. All rights reserved.

ISBN: 978-1-64938-014-2
RoseKidz® reorder #380142
Product Code R50028
RELIGION/Christian Ministry/Children

Printed in the United States of America
Printed April 2021

Table of Contents

Introduction 7
How to Use This Book 8

Holidays

Epiphany
A Gift for the Magi... 9
The Magi Followed the Star 10
The Visit of the Magi 11

Valentine's Day
Greater Love... 12
Do You Love Me?... 13
"Hearty" Accordion Person 14
Weekly Valentine Devotions 16
Heart Puzzle... 17
Lovable Mice.. 18
Pass the Hearts Game 19
Valentine's Day Symbols 20
Saint Valentine 21
God's Gift of Love 22
God's Love for Us 23
God's Word Teaches about Love 24
Heart of Stone 25
The Eyes of Our Hearts 26
Jesus Is King of Our Hearts 27
God First Loved Us... 28
We Are Living Valentines................................. 29
Share the Love of Christ.................................. 30
Basket of Hearts 32

Purim
Celebrate Like Royalty..................................... 34

St. Patrick's Day
Shamrock Garden 37

Palm Sunday
Hosanna to the King 38
Riding on a Donkey 39
Praise Jesus 40
Jesus' Triumphant Entry.................................. 41
Dot-to-Dot Donkey.. 42

Good Friday
The Way of the Cross 43
Cross Sun Catchers.. 44
New Life 46
Sign on the Cross 47
Jesus Died So We Can Live.............................. 48
A God of Promises 49
Jesus Is Not Ashamed of Us 50
Jesus on the Cross 51

Easter
Easter Story Object Lesson............................. 52
Easter Newspaper 54
Easter Lilies Crossword 55
Easter A-Cross-Tic... 56
Resurrection A-Cross-Tic 57
Our Easter Traditions 58
The Sunrise and the Risen Son 59
Symbols of Easter.. 60
Jesus Is Risen 61
Colors of Easter... 62
He Makes All Things New................................ 63
Victory Over Death.. 64
Jesus Is Lord of All 66
Angelic Announcement 68
Happy Easter 70
Celebrate Easter.. 72

Passover
Protected by God... 74
Stained Glass Window 75

Pentecost
- Stained Glass Church 76
- Pentecost Celebration 78
- The Fruit of the Holy Spirit 79
- Search for God's Word 80

National Day of Prayer
- Five-Finger Prayer 81
- Prayer Code 82

Shavuot (Feast of Weeks)
- God's Promise to the Israelites 83
- Harvest Festival 84

Rosh Hashanah (Jewish New Year)
- Shout It Out Shofar 85

Sukkot (Feast of Tabernacles)
- Feast of Tabernacles 86

Yom Kippur (Day of Atonement)
- Prayer of Atonement 87

Reformation Day
- Reformation Day Celebration 88
- Luther's Rose 89

Thanksgiving
- Turkey Tom 90
- A Grand Old Gobbler 91
- Hanging Horn of Plenty 93
- Thanksgiving Hand Card 96
- Thanksgiving Celebration 97
- Thanksgiving Crossword 98
- Thanksgiving Code 99
- Abundant Blessings 100
- Color Me Turkey: Younger Elementary 101
- Color Me Turkey: Older Elementary 102
- The Pilgrims 103
- A Thanksgiving Feast 104
- We Celebrate Thanksgiving 105
- Harvest Time Abundance 106
- Happy Thanksgiving 107
- Thanksgiving Care 109
- The First Thanksgiving 111

Hanukkah (Festival of Lights)
- Festival of Lights 113
- Dreidel Game 114

Advent
- Advent Giving Tree 116
- Family Advent Wreath 118

Christmas
- Angels Appear 119
- The Candy Cane Story 120
- Sweet Candy Canes Bouquet 121
- Circle of Love 123
- Candle Wreath 124
- Pop Up Nativity 126
- Christmas Gift Pockets 128
- Christmas Winter Fun 129
- Christmas Tree Puzzle 130
- Special Visitor Code 131
- Christmas Poem 132
- Wise Men Maze 133
- Shepherds Search for Jesus 134
- Why Jesus Came Maze 135
- Christmas Plan-Ahead Program 136
- Christmas Celebration 137
- Prophecies of the Messiah 138
- The Symbol of the Candy Cane 139
- Christmas Traditions 140
- Christmas Symbols 141
- The Angel Visits Mary 142
- The Angel Visits Joseph 143
- Journey to Bethlehem 144
- At the Inn 145

Born in Bethlehem 146
Jesus' Birth Announcement..................... 147
An Angel Visits the Shepherds 148
Baby Jesus in the Manger 149
Celebrate Christmas Every Day.................... 150
Jesus' Birthday.. 151
The Real Reason 152
The Angel's Announcement 154
Christmas Around the World........................ 156

Special Days

New Year's Day
Pottery Puzzle.. 158
Spiritual Inventory.................................. 159
The Promised Land 160
Happy New Year.................................... 161

Martin Luther King Day
My Dreams Mobile.................................. 162
Martin Luther King's Dream.................... 163

President's Day
Honest Abe Story.................................. 164
Truthful George Story 165
Stately Silhouettes................................. 166
President's Day Celebration 169

Earth Day
Paper Cone Lilies 170
Seeds Bring Forth Life 172
Earth Day Word Search 173
Caretakers of the Earth 174
New Life in Christ.................................. 175

Teacher Appreciation Day
Teacher Day Celebration 176
Thank You, Teacher 177
Teacher Feature................................... 178

Mother's Day
Coupon Book of Promises 179
I Love My Mom Card 180
Mother's Day Poem 181
Bible Mothers Quiz................................ 182
Mothers Are God's Masterpiece 183
Sarah Was a Woman of Faith 184
Mother of Faith..................................... 185
Grocery Store Helper............................ 186
Jochebed, Miriam, and Moses 187
Flowers for Mother................................ 188
Happy Mother's Day 189
Mother's Arms 191

Victoria Day
A Royal Birthday................................... 193

Memorial Day
Medal of Peace 194

Father's Day
Prodigal Son Story................................ 195
I Love My Dad Card 196
Dad's Key Rack 197
Bible Fathers Quiz................................. 198
Heavenly Father Crossword.................. 199
We Are Children of God........................ 200
Adopted into God's Family 201
Jesus and His Father Joseph................ 202
Adam Tells His Son about God 203
Teaching about God.............................204
Abraham's Big Family 205
We Are Abraham's Family 206
Happy Father's Day...............................207
Father's Wisdom 209

Juneteenth
Juneteenth Prayer Chain...................... 211
Code of Chains.....................................212

Independence Day
- Fashionable Flags 213
- Firework Rockets 215
- Celebration Crossword 216
- What Makes a Nation Great? 217
- My Fourth of July Day 218
- Happy Birthday, America 219
- The Truth Will Set You Free 220
- Park Picnic 221

Labor Day
- A Mind at Work 222
- Willing Worker Maze 223
- Honor the Sabbath Day 224

Grandparents Day
- Grandparents Day Celebration 225
- Our Best Memories 227
- Happy Grandparents Day 228
- We Love with Our Actions 229

Columbus Day
- Texture Ship 230

Pastor Appreciation Day
- Hands Down the Best Pastor 232
- Pastor Crossword 233

Halloween Alternatives
Harvest Party
- Corny Craft 234
- Crayon Leaf Placemats 236
- Sweet Treats 238
- Happy Pumpkin Word Search 239

Noah's Ark Party
- Noah's Ark Celebration 240

Light of the World Party
- Light-of-the-World Celebration 243
- Missionary Mission 244

For additional Halloween Alternatives, see Reformation Day activities.

Children's Day
- Children's Talent Show 245
- Let the Children Come 246

Boxing Day
- The Greatest Gift Ever Given 247

Kwanzaa
- Seven Principles Search 248

Celebrations
Birthdays
- Birthday Thoughts 249
- Birthday Bear 250

Graduation Day
- Graduation Caps 252

Vacation
- Vacation Books 253

Sabbath
See "Honor the Sabbath Day" under Labor Day, page 224

Introduction

As Christians, we strive to keep God at the center of our daily lives. Special occasions should be no different. With this activity-packed book, you can easily occupy any child or group of children ages five to ten with important information about why we celebrate these holidays, special days, and celebrations. We hope that this resource will help you create lessons that are a blast for you to teach and exciting for kids to complete, all while keep it centered on God and his Word, the Bible.

How This Book Is Organized

The table of contents is divided into holidays, special days, and celebrations. If you don't find the occasion you're looking for under one category, check the others!

Holidays

Holidays are holy days that have direct connections to the Christian faith. These are days that were either celebrated in the Bible (Shavuot, Sukkot, Yom Kippur, etc.), celebrate an event from the Bible (Easter, Christmas, etc.), or celebrate saints or religious movements (St. Patrick's Day, Reformation Day etc.). Though some of these holy days may have become secularized, this book aims to refocus every occasion on God with reproducible activity pages for children ages five to ten.

Special Days

Special days are celebratory occasions that are not religious by nature, but this book has created some faith-filled connections to make God the center of every celebration. For example, President's Day honors Abraham Lincoln and George Washington. Both these leaders were honored for their honesty, faith, and sacrifices for the country. Teach children how to be an honest leader on this special day.

Note: Special day celebrations are flexible and many can be used across other occasions.

Celebrations

Celebrations are occasions that do not fall on a specific day of the year because they are different for everyone. These include birthdays, graduation days, and vacations days.

How to Use This Book

Each occasion includes a variety of reproducible activities including stories with discussion questions, crafts, games, party celebration ideas, activity pages (word searches, crosswords, codes, mazes, etc.) and coloring pages.

What You Need and Preparation

Before class, gather the items from the "What You Need" list and follow the instructions under "Preparation." If a page does not include a "What You Need" or "Preparation" section, photocopy the page making one for each child and hand out crayons or markers for children to write or draw on the page.

What It's All About

Read the bold text to the children so that they have a context for the activity. As a general rule of thumb in this book, any bold text should be spoken out loud by the teacher.

What To Do

Follow the easy step-by-step instructions to complete the activity. Some activity pages (word searches, crosswords, codes, mazes, etc.) and coloring pages may not include this section because of space limitations. In that case, you'll find the instructions either within the "What It's All About" section or directly underneath.

Optional Take-Home Resources

Photocopy the codes, coloring pages, crosswords, mazes, or word searches as take-home resources so that children can share what they learned with their families.

A Gift for the Magi

What can I offer the Lord for all he has done for me? **Psalm 116:12**

What You Need
• Crayons or markers • Glue • Shoebox, one for each child • Paper • Straw or Easter grass

Preparation
Photocopy this page, making one for each child.

What It's All About
Epiphany is traditionally celebrated on January 6. It is a time to remember when the Magi journeyed to the birthplace of baby Jesus. The Magi brought gifts of gold, frankincense, and myrrh to Jesus. In many countries, children fill boxes with grass or straw the night before Epiphany. This grass is for the Magi's camels. The children then place these boxes under their beds, in hopes that the Magi will leave gifts in place of the grass or straw.

This special day gives you the opportunity to think about what gifts you can give Jesus. He is no longer a baby in a manger, but he grew up, gave his life so that we would not have to pay the penalty for our sins, rose from the dead, and now lives in Heaven. Jesus wants to receive gifts from us today. He wants us to love him, to talk with him, to obey him, and to read God's Word.

What To Do
1. Color the Magi and memory verse.
2. Glue the Magi and memory verse to the lid of the shoebox.
3. Decorate the shoebox with crayons or markers.
4. On a piece of paper, draw a picture of what you'd like to give Jesus for the new year.
5. Fill the shoebox with straw or Easter grass.
6. Place the picture on top of the straw or Easter grass inside the box. Put the lid on the box.
7. Place the gift box in your room as a reminder of what you've given to Jesus.

"What can I offer the Lord for all he has done for me?"

Psalm 116:12

The Magi Followed the Star

Wise men from eastern lands arrived in Jerusalem, asking, "Where is the newborn king of the Jews? We saw his star as it rose, and we have come to worship him." **Matthew 2:1–2**

What It's All About

Magi, sometimes called wise men, followed the star to find Jesus. These Magi studied stars and realized that a new king had been born for the Jews. They possibly traveled thousands of miles to Jerusalem. Color the picture of the wise men following the star to see baby Jesus.

The Visit of the Magi

[The wise men] entered the house and saw the child with his mother, Mary, and they bowed down and worshiped him. Then they opened their treasure chests and gave him gifts of gold, frankincense, and myrrh. **Matthew 2:11**

What It's All About

King Herod sent the Magi to Bethlehem because it was the prophesied birthplace of the Messiah. When the Magi arrived, they caused a stir among the people by asking for the newborn king of the Jews. Then the Magi found Jesus. They worshiped Jesus and gave him three kinds of gifts.

Decorate the boxes that contained the three kinds of gifts, and draw bricks on the house. Color the picture.

Epiphany • 11

Greater Love

There is no greater love than to lay down one's life for one's friends. **John 15:13**

What It's All About

It is fun to send and receive valentines. We send them to express our love and friendship to others. Sometimes you may select a very special one if it is for a person you really love, like your mom or dad. You might send silly ones to your friends.

There are many kinds of love. There is a *romantic* kind of love that you feel for a boyfriend or girlfriend. There is a *devotion* kind of love that you feel for your parents, brothers, and sisters. They are your family, so that is a tender and gentle love. But when you say you "love" pizza, that is a totally different sort of love. It only means you really like to eat pizza. We don't love pizza in the same way we love people.

The Bible says that we are to have a compassionate type of love for others around us. This is a caring kind of love. We should care when people around us are hurting. We should try to help them.

Christ is the ultimate example of compassionate love. He was willing to give his own life for us. There can be no greater love than that!

Let's color this picture as a reminder of Jesus' great love and how he wants us to love others. Write answers to the questions on the lines provided.

Discussion Questions

1. Why do we send valentines?

   _____

2. Name the different kinds of love.

   _____

Do You Love Me?

Show love to the LORD your God by walking in his ways and holding tightly to him. **Deuteronomy 11:22**

Based on John 21:15–17

One day Jesus had breakfast with his disciples. Jesus asked Simon Peter if he loved him. Of course, Peter replied that he did. Jesus asked him again if he truly loved him, and again Peter said yes. Then Jesus told him, "Feed my sheep."

Jesus did not have a flock of sheep that he wanted Peter to water and feed. He was talking about taking care of people. He wanted Peter to love him enough to do whatever he asked. On Valentine's Day, we make a special effort to show people that we love and appreciate them.

Let's color this picture to remember this story about love. Write answers to the questions on the lines provided.

Discussion Questions

1. Why did Jesus ask Peter if he loved him?

   _____

2. Who are Jesus' sheep?

   _____

3. How can we show Jesus that we truly love him?

   _____

Valentine's Day • 13

© 2021 Rose Publishing, LLC. Permission to photocopy granted to original purchaser only. *The Super-Sized Book of Holidays, Special Days, & Celebrations.*

"Hearty" Accordion Person

If you look for me wholeheartedly, you will find me. **Jeremiah 29:13**

What You Need
- "Hearty" Patterns (p. 15) • Scissors • Red, white, and black construction paper
- Crayons or markers • Ruler • Glue • Hole punch • Red yarn

Preparation
Photocopy "Hearty" Patterns, making one pattern for each child. Prepare a sample completed project.

What It's All About
When you love something, you dedicate a lot of time to it. Maybe you love to dance, play sports, read, or sing. When you do these things with your whole heart, you get better at them.

God wants you to look for him with all your heart. That means he wants your eyes focused on studying the Bible, your mouth focused on speaking kindly, and your body focused on acting respectfully. Today, we'll make a heart person to remind us to seek and love God with our whole heart.

What To Do

1. Using the patterns, cut one large heart from red paper, four medium hearts from red paper, two small hearts from white paper, and four mini hearts from black paper (Note: When making the large heart, fold red paper in half and trace the half large heart template over the fold.).

> You will not need to use the "regular" sized heart pattern.

2. Write the memory verse on one side of the largest heart.
3. Assemble the face as shown in the illustration; place two white hearts as the eyes; place two black hearts over the white hearts as the pupils; place the last two black hearts as the nose and mouth.
4. Cut four 1-inch strips of white construction paper. Two of the strips should be 7 inches long and two should be 11 inches long. Accordion-fold all the strips.
5. Glue the two shorter strips to the upper-side of the large heart for arms. Glue one small red heart to the other end of each "arm" for hands.
6. Glue the two longer strips near the point of the heart for legs. Glue a small red heart to the other end of each strip for feet.
7. Punch a hole in the top center of the heart top.
8. Thread an 8-inch piece of red yarn through the hole. Tie in a loop for hanging.

"Hearty" Patterns

Valentine's Day • 15

Weekly Valentine Devotions

Love each other in the same way I have loved you. **John 15:12**

What You Need
- Bible • "Hearty" Patterns (p. 15) • Red construction paper • Scissors • Stapler • Crayons or markers

Preparation
Photocopy "Hearty" Patterns onto red construction paper, making two patterns for each child.

What It's All About
Valentine's Day is all about showing your friends and family how much you love them. The memory verse tells us to love God the same way that God loves you. But if you don't know how God loves you, how can you love others? Today we are going to make a craft that is full of verses about God's love. Each day this week, you can learn about God's love and how to love others better.

What To Do
1. Using the patterns, cut out two large red hearts and eight regular red hearts.
2. Staple the two large red hearts together along the sides and bottom. This is the heart envelope.
3. Write one of the verse references listed below on each of the eight regular hearts.
4. Place the verse hearts inside the heart envelope.
5. Each day this week, take one verse heart from the heart envelope.
6. Look up the verse and read it out loud.

Scripture References:
- John 13:34
- John 15:10
- John 14:23–24
- John 13:35
- John 15:12
- Romans 8:28
- Psalm 18:1–2

Heart Puzzle

Love the LORD your God with all your heart, all your soul, all your strength, and all your mind. **Luke 10:27**

What You Need
- Colored paper • Scissors • Glue

Preparation
Photocopy this page onto colored paper, making one for each child.

What It's All About
On Valentine's Day, we think of who we love most of all. Who are we supposed to love most of all? How much should we love him?

What To Do
1. Cut out the heart and the pieces with words on them.
2. Glue the pieces into the correct place on the heart.

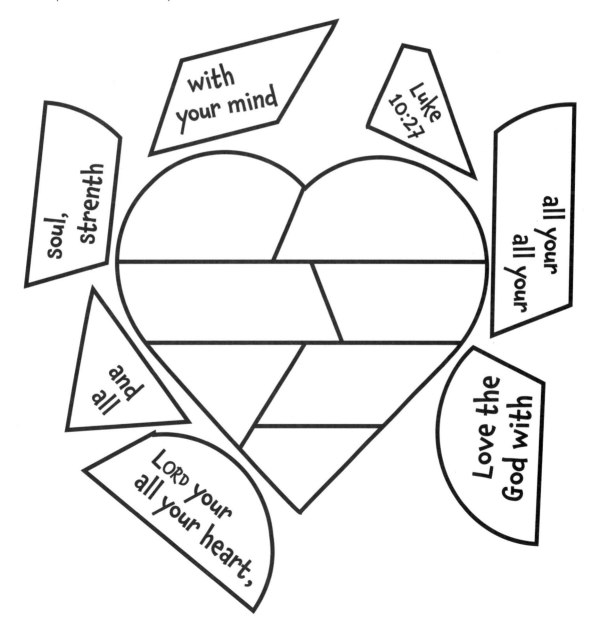

Valentine's Day • 17

Lovable Mice

You care for people and animals alike, O LORD. How precious is your unfailing love, O God! **Psalm 36:6–7**

What You Need

- Scissors • White, pink, and black construction paper • Ruler • Gray or white yarn
- Glue • Crayons or markers • Cotton balls • Hole punch

Preparation

Photocopy this page, making one pattern for each child. Prepare a sample completed project.

What To Do

1. Use the patterns to trace and cut one large heart from white construction paper and two small hearts from pink construction paper.
2. Fold the large heart in half.
3. Cut a 6-inch strand of gray or white yarn.
4. Glue the yarn to the inside fold of the heart at the large end.
5. Write the memory verse on one of the flat sides of the heart.
6. Gently pull cotton balls to loosen the fibers. Stuff a small amount inside the heart and glue along the edges to close them.
7. Punch two black eyes from construction paper with the hole punch.
8. Glue one black eye to each side at the pointed end.
9. For each side, fold pink hearts, gluing one heart to each side of the body for ears.
10. Color the pointed tip black with a marker for a nose.

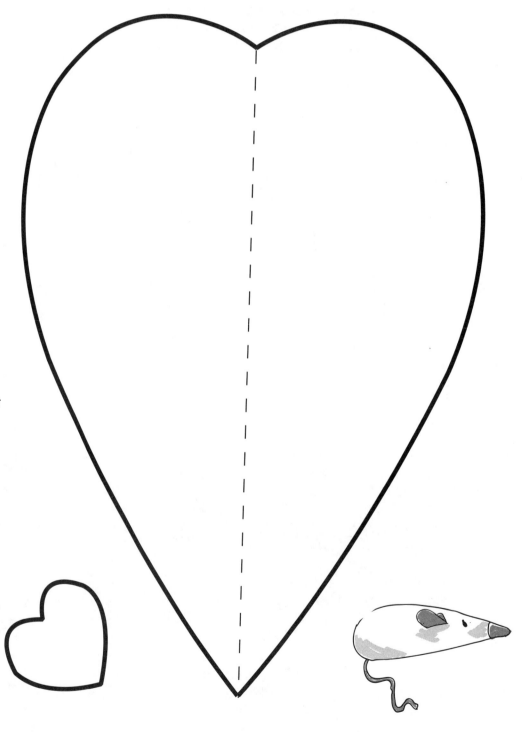

18 • Valentine's Day

Pass the Hearts Game

May the Lord make your love for one another and for all people grow and overflow, just as our love for you overflows. **1 Thessalonians 3:12**

What You Need
- Resealable plastic bag • Conversation hearts candy

Preparation
Photocopy this page, making one for each child.

What It's All About
Valentine's Day is a day for sharing love. Love isn't always a mushy gushy feeling. Sharing love also means being kind, patient, respectful, helpful, and more! How can you show love to others every day?

What To Do
1. Players make a large circle around the leader.
2. The first player holds a securely-tied bag of conversation hearts candy.
3. As the children pass the bag of candy from player to player, the leader will sing the following lyrics to the tune of "Where Oh Where Has My Little Dog Gone?":

    Where, oh where has the candy gone?
    Oh where, oh where can it be?
    With the bag tied tight for the party tonight,
    Oh where, oh where can it be?

4. Sing song all the way through at least once. Then, suddenly stop singing in the middle of a line or word. Whoever is holding the bag of candy when the singing stops must go into the circle with the leader.
5. Continue until only one child is not standing with the leader. This child recites, or chooses someone else to recite, the memory verse.
6. When the game is over, players share the candy, with the final player having first choice.

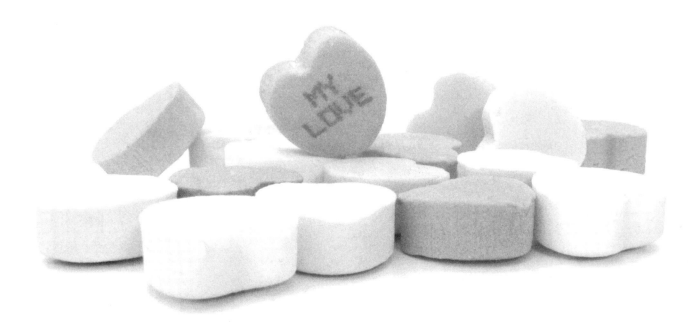

Valentine's Day Symbols

Three things will last forever—faith, hope, and love—and the greatest of these is love. **1 Corinthians 13:13**

What It's All About

The heart is the symbol of love. Valentine's Day is the day to show our love toward others. The festivities of Valentine's Day include parties, giving and receiving valentines, and enjoying treats. Jesus tells us that there is no greater love than laying down your life for a friend. And that is exactly what Jesus did for us. Now that is a love worth celebrating! Let's celebrate Jesus' great love by coloring this picture of things that remind us of Valentine's Day.

Saint Valentine

A friend is always loyal, and a brother is born to help in time of need. **Proverbs 17:17**

What It's All About

Legend says that Saint Valentine was a Christian priest who was killed for performing marriages for Roman lovers. At that time in history, many young Roman men refused to join the army because of their dedication to their wives and families. The emperor banned all new marriages and engagements in Rome, but Valentine refused to obey. So he was arrested and put in prison.

Valentine became friends with the jailer's daughter, who showed him kindness. The day before his execution on February 14, he thanked her for her friendship in a note signed, "Your Valentine." No matter how true legends are, Valentine's Day helps us focus on love for each other. Jesus is the greatest example of love that this world has ever known.

Color the picture. Draw flowers and a forest of trees.

God's Gift of Love

We know how much God loves us, and we have put our trust in his love. **1 John 4:16**

What It's All About

Our God is a God of love. He loved us, but our sins kept us separated from him. God's love for us is so great that he gave us a Savior. That is love in action! Jesus is God's gift of love to us, but it is still up to us to accept it.

Color this picture to remember God's gift of love. If you haven't before, tell Jesus you want to receive his gift of eternal life.

God's Love for Us

God showed his great love for us by sending Christ to die for us while we were still sinners. **Romans 5:8**

What It's All About

Jesus died for us while we were sinners. He did not wait until we were good enough, because we can never be good enough to earn salvation. Sin deserves punishment. Jesus paid the punishment for sin for all of us. As Jesus died, he knew it was for people like us. He had the power to save himself from the pain and anguish at any moment, but instead he obeyed his Father.

Color the picture and draw a picture of yourself inside the heart.

God's Word Teaches about Love

Loving God means keeping his commandments, and his commandments are not burdensome. **1 John 5:3**

What It's All About

Jesus says that if we love him, we will keep his commandments. So how do we know what his commandments are? The Bible is the only true source for God's commandments. It was written by ordinary people, but God inspired their writing. Therefore, we can read it, trust it, and learn from it.

Look up the verses inside the hearts to see how God wants us to love. Then, color the page.

24 • Valentine's Day

Heart of Stone

I will give you a new heart, and I will put a new spirit in you. **Ezekiel 36:26**

What It's All About

God changes hearts. He promises to give you a new heart when you accept Jesus as Lord and Savior. This new heart will help you to be kind and loving toward others. Your old heart is like a heart of stone—not very loving at all. God gives you his Spirit, too, to help you know what is right and wrong so you can obey him.

Color this picture of a stone heart and a new heart filled with the Holy Spirit as a reminder of Ezekiel 36:26.

The Eyes of Our Hearts

I pray that your hearts will be flooded with light so that you can understand the confident hope he has given to those he called. **Ephesians 1:18**

What It's All About

In Ephesians 1:18, Paul prays for all Christians to understand God's Word. That is why he prays that the eyes of their hearts will be open to learning. We don't really have eyes in our hearts, but from our hearts come our feelings and how we treat other people. Our hearts can be kind or unkind. When we are willing to obey God and do what his Word says, the eyes of our hearts are open to him.

Draw eyes on all the hearts and color the picture.

Jesus Is King of Our Hearts

At just the right time Christ will be revealed from heaven by the blessed and only almighty God, the King of all kings and the Lord of all lords. **1 Timothy 6:15**

What It's All About

To make Jesus King of our hearts, we have to believe in him and accept his free gift of salvation. Then we will want to please our King, learn from the Bible, and do our best to do what it says.

Draw a crown on Jesus' head. Then color the picture.

God First Loved Us

Dear friends, since God loved us that much, we surely ought to love each other. **1 John 4:11**

What It's All About

We can never do anything or be good enough to earn God's love. He loves us no matter what happens! Our all-powerful God loves us even when we sin. His love for us helps us to love others. We can do that because of the Holy Spirit, who gives us the power to love all people, especially those who are not very lovable.

Color this picture of things that remind us of Jesus and his amazing love. It can remind us to love others, too.

We Are Living Valentines

Live clean, innocent lives as children of God, shining like bright lights in a world full of crooked and perverse people. **Philippians 2:15**

What It's All About

Everyone loves to receive valentines. They let us know how much we are loved. We can be a living valentine every day of the year, not just on Valentine's Day, by doing what the Bible tells us—to love others. Sometimes it is not easy to love others, especially if they are not very nice to us. But when we do, we are like shining stars in the dark of night.

Draw more hearts, trace over "Jesus Loves You" and give the valentine to someone who has shown kindness toward you.

Share the Love of Christ

Dear friends, let us continue to love one another, for love comes from God. Anyone who loves is a child of God and knows God. **1 John 4:7**

What You Need
- Bouquet Valentine (p. 31) • Crayons or markers

Preparation
Photocopy this page and Bouquet Valentine making one of each page for each child.

What It's All About
Valentine's Day is a great time to share the love of Christ by doing kind things for people. The simple act of sending valentines lets people know that you love them and that God loves them.

What To Do
1. Color the pictures on both pages.
2. On the page that's a valentine, draw flowers in the bouquet and give the valentine to someone for Valentine's Day.

30 • Valentine's Day

Bouquet Valentine

To: _____

From: _____

This Valentine wish is full of love
That only God gives us from above.

Wishing you a Jesus-filled Valentine's Day!

Basket of Hearts

Love each other deeply with all your heart. **1 Peter 1:22**

What You Need
- Basket Valentine (p. 33) • Crayons or markers

Preparation
Photocopy this page and Basket Valentine, making one of each page for each child.

What It's All About
Have you ever made and given cookies to express your love or care toward others? We show people Jesus' love when we do little acts of kindness. Sending cards or letters is one great way to do this. Can you think of someone to whom you could send a valentine?

What To Do
1. Color both pages.
2. On Basket Valentine, draw hearts inside the basket that the puppy is holding.
3. Give the Basket Valentine to a special friend.

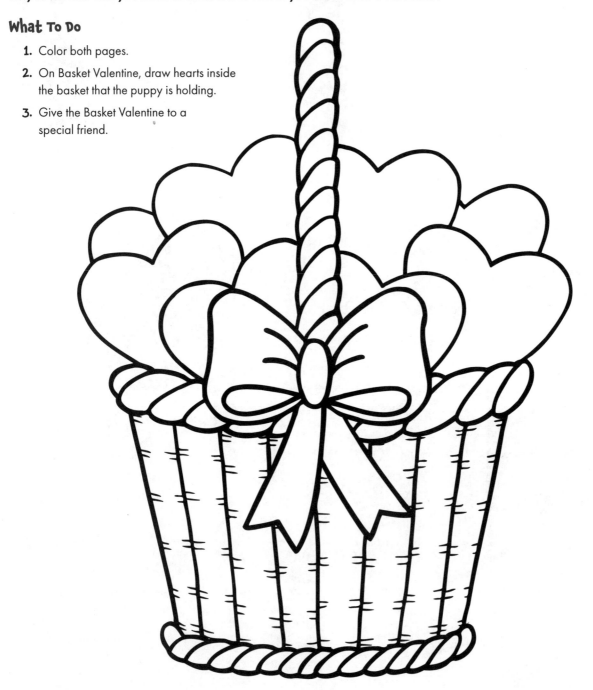

32 • Valentine's Day

Basket Valentine

To: _____

From: _____

This basket of love
Comes along your way
To wish you the best
On this Valentine's Day!

Celebrate Like Royalty

Come, everyone! Clap your hands! Shout to God with joyful praise! **Psalm 47:1**

What You Need
- Queen Mask and King Mask (pp. 35–36) • Scissors • Crayons or markers
- Decorative elements (glitter, stickers, gem stones, etc.) • Hole punch • String or yarn

Preparation
Photocopy one Queen Mask for each girl and one King Mask for each boy. Make a few extras in case of guests.

What It's All About
Purim is a holiday celebrating Queen Esther and her courageous act to save her people. Queen Esther's husband, King Xerxes, was tricked by Haman, his second-in-command. Haman hated the Jews and tricked the King into signing a death warrant to kill the Jews in Persia. King Xerxes didn't know that Queen Esther was Jewish.

At a special banquet for the King and Haman, Queen Esther bravely asked the King to spare her and her people. King Xerxes listened to Queen Esther's advice. The Jews were saved!

Many Jewish children celebrate Purim by dressing up in costumes, listening to the story of Esther, shaking noise makers when Haman's name is mentioned, and eating Hamantashen. Hamantashen are triangular-shaped cookies which represent Haman's second-in-command hat.

Today, we'll dress up like Queen Esther and King Xerxes.

What To Do
1. Cut out the mask.
2. Decorate the mask with crayons, markers, and other decorative elements.
3. Punch a hole on the sides of the mask where indicated.
4. Wrap string or yarn around head to measure and then cut correct length.
5. Tie string or yarn through the holes and secure around head.

Queen Mask

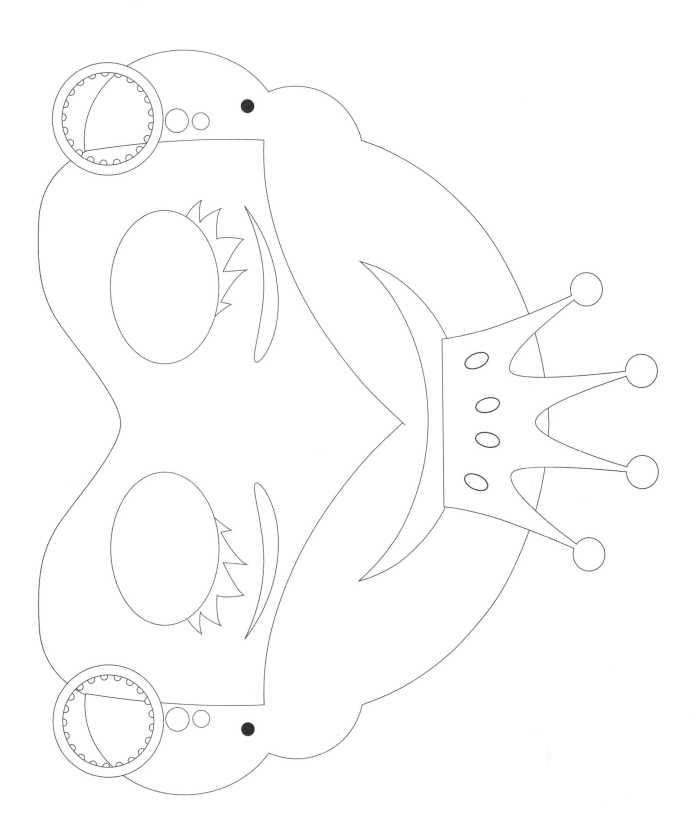

Purim • 35

King Mask

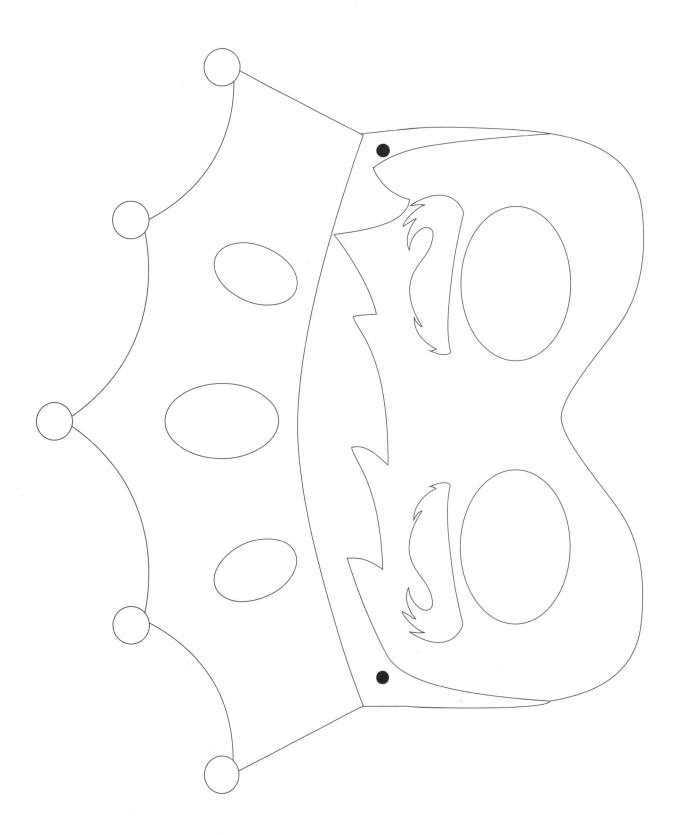

Shamrock Garden

Grow in the grace and knowledge of our Lord. **2 Peter 3:18**

What You Need
• Green construction paper • Scissors • Glue • Tape • Green pipe cleaners • Crayons or markers

Preparation
Photocopy this page onto green construction paper, making one pattern for each child.

What It's All About
On March 17 people honor St. Patrick, the patron saint of Ireland, who died on this date over 1,500 years ago. St. Patrick was known for his love of learning. Most people of his time were not educated. So St. Patrick taught all the people he baptized how to read and write. These skills are very important for those who wish to learn about God and his Word. Because the shamrock is the national flower of Ireland, it is an ancient custom to wear a shamrock or a bit of green on St. Patrick's Day in memory of St. Patrick.

What To Do

1. Cut three hearts out of the green construction paper you've been given.
2. Write three words of the memory verse on each heart. Or write the verse reference on one of the hearts.
3. Glue the points of the three hearts together to make a shamrock. Let dry.
4. Tape a green pipe cleaner to the back of the shamrock.
5. Twist the pipe cleaner around a button on your shirt or around your wrist as a reminder to read the Bible.
6. Repeat, making more shamrocks as interest and supplies last.

Hosanna to the King

Come, let us sing to the LORD! Let us shout joyfully to the Rock of our salvation. **Psalm 95:1**

What It's All About

When Jesus and his disciples were near Jerusalem, Jesus sent two disciples to get a colt. He said that it would be tied beside it's mother, and they were free to take it. The disciples obeyed, found the small colt, and brought it back to Jesus.

Why do you think Jesus chose to ride a donkey? Horses were larger and more powerful creatures. Jesus could have arrived on a valiant steed. But Jesus did not want to show off his power. The Roman soldiers rode horses through the streets to show their power over the people. Although Jesus was more powerful than the Romans, he came as a servant.

Jesus rode a donkey to fulfill a prophecy. It was a sign to the people of Jerusalem that Jesus was the true servant king. He came to sacrifice his life for his people, although many people did not realize that at the time.

The disciples threw their coats over the donkey for Jesus to sit on. Then, he rode into Jerusalem. The people were so excited! They threw their coats down on the ground for the donkey to walk on. They waved palm branches in the air singing "Hosanna to the King!" Today, we celebrate Jesus' triumphant return to Jerusalem as Palm Sunday. Color the picture and answer the questions.

Discussion Questions

1. Why was it important that Jesus arrive on a donkey instead of a horse?

   _____

   _____

2. Why do you think the people were excited to see Jesus?

   _____

   _____

Riding on a Donkey

Tell the people of Jerusalem, "Look, your King is coming to you. He is humble, riding on a donkey—riding on a donkey's colt." **Matthew 21:5**

What You Need

• White cardstock • Gray or brown crayons or markers • Scissors • Green construction paper • Glue

Preparation

Photocopy this page onto cardstock, making one for each child.

What It's All About

In the story of Jesus' triumphant entry into Jerusalem (Mark 11:1—10), we often forget something very important. We may be so busy thinking of the people who sang praises and spread their garments before the Lord that we forget the little donkey that carried him into the city.

In Bible times, when a leader rode into town on a horse, it was symbol of war. If a leader rode in on a donkey, it was a symbol of peace. Jesus' riding a donkey was a sign to all the people that he was coming in peace, not as a warrior to overthrow the government. This also fulfilled the prophecy that the Messiah would arrive in Jerusalem on a donkey (see Zechariah 9:9).

Whenever you see a donkey, remember how Jesus refused to become an earthly king and instead died on a cross to save us from our sins.

What To Do

1. Color the donkey gray or brown.
2. Cut out the donkey and legs, including the small slits on the body and legs.
3. Fit the donkey body onto the legs so that it stands up.
4. Draw a palm branch on a sheet of green construction paper.
5. Cut out the palm branch.
6. Glue the donkey to the palm branch. Let dry.
7. Put the donkey in your room as a reminder of Jesus' entry into Jerusalem.

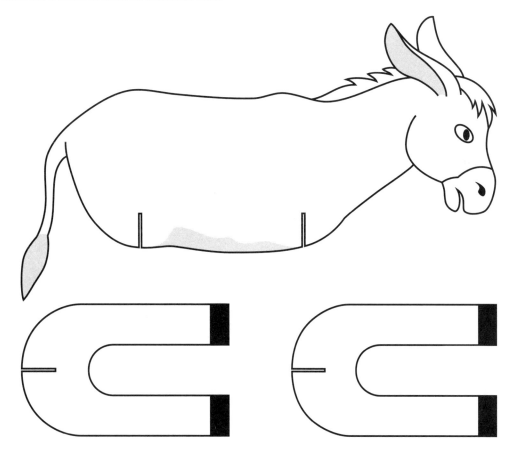

Palm Sunday • 39

Praise Jesus

I will praise the Lord at all times. I will constantly speak his praises. **Psalm 34:1**

What You Need
- Crayons or markers

Preparation
Photocopy this page, making one for each child.

What It's All About
On Palm Sunday, the people of Jerusalem praised Jesus by waving palm branches and spreading their coats on the road.

What To Do
Use the words describing Jesus from the word box to fill in the blanks. Some letters are filled in to get you started.

Word Box

| Friend | Priest | Savior |
| King | Redeemer | Son of God |

P _ _ _ _ _

_ R _ _ _ _

_ A _ _ _ _

_ _ I _ _

S _ _ _ _ _ _ _

_ E _ _ _ _ _

Jesus' Triumphant Entry

_____ *will be known as "The Throne of the* Lord.*" All nations will come there to honor the* Lord. **Jeremiah 3:17**

What You Need
- Crayons or markers

Preparation
Photocopy this page, making one for each child.

What It's All About
Jesus knew when and where he was going to die. Palm Sunday celebrates Jesus' entry into the capital of Judea. It was a joyful celebration as Jesus entered the city on the colt of a donkey. The people welcomed him waving palm branches and spreading their coats on the road. The name of the famous city Jesus entered is missing from our verse. These clues will help you figure out what it is.

What To Do
1. Read the clues and write the correct letters on the lines.
2. Write the complete word on the last line.

In JESTER but not in STEER... _____

In BEAT but not in BAT... _____

In WRAP but not in PAW... _____

In GLUE but not in LEG... _____

In BOAST but not in BOAT... _____

In PAINT but not in PINT... _____

In LOVER but not in ROVE... _____

In TRACE but not in CART... _____

In PALM but not in PAL... _____

Jesus rode on a colt into what city?

_____

Dot-to-Dot Donkey

Blessings on the King who comes in the name of the LORD! Peace in heaven, and glory in the highest heaven! Luke 19:38

What You Need
- Crayons or markers

Preparation
Photocopy this page, making one for each child.

What It's All About
When Jesus arrived in Jerusalem, he did not ride a horse. A horse was a sign of power. Many Roman soldiers rode horses through the crowded streets. They'd shove people aside to make room for the generals and tax collectors. Jesus was more powerful than the Romans, but he chose to ride a lowly humble animal instead. It showed that he came to serve the people. He was a very different kind of king.

What To Do
1. Starting at number one, connect the dots to discover what animal Jesus rode into Jerusalem.
2. Draw Jesus riding on the animal.

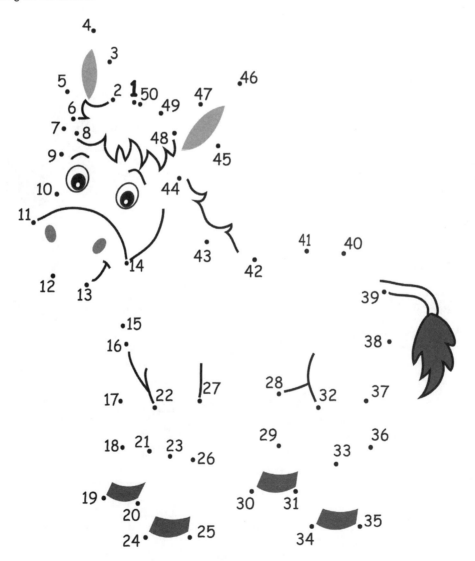

The Way of the Cross

I am the light of the world. If you follow me, you won't have to walk in darkness, because you will have the light that leads to life. **John 8:12**

What It's All About

A little girl lived in a small village at the edge of a great forest. She loved to pick flowers that grew along the border of the dense underbrush.

In the middle of the village stood a white clapboard church with a tall steeple. On top of the steeple was a metal cross. The little girl's mom had told her to always look for the cross and never wander so far away that she could not see it.

One day as the girl was exploring, she entered deeper into the woods than she realized. Suddenly, she looked around and didn't know which path led out of the forest. After frantically searching for a few minutes, she sat down and began to cry. Then, as she lifted her tear-stained eyes, the sun sent a glint her way. As she rose and slowly walked in the direction of the cross, she saw the cross gleaming in the distance. Now she knew how to get home!

The cross on which Christ died has become a way out of the darkness for millions of people. When we look to the cross we will be able to find our way to our heavenly home. We must never lose sight of the cross.

As we celebrate on Easter, let's color this picture to remember Jesus' great sacrifice. Write answers to the questions on the lines provided.

Discussion Questions

1. How did the cross lead the little girl home?

   _____

   _____

2. How does the cross lead people out of darkness?

   _____

   _____

3. Who promised "a way out" for us?

   _____

   _____

Cross Sun Catchers

Jesus told him, "I am the way, the truth, and the life. No one can come to the Father except through me." **John 14:6**

What You Need

- Cross Template (p. 45) • Scissors • Colored card stock, one sheet for each child
- Glue • Clear plastic transparency sheet, one for each child
- Black permanent marker • Colored permanent markers
- Hole punch • Suction cup hook

Preparation

Photocopy this page and the Cross Template, making enough copies for each child to have one cross pattern and one flower pattern. Prepare a completed project for children to reference.

What It's All About

This craft will remind us that Jesus' death brought spiritual light to the world. Nothing is hidden from Jesus. He sees everything that you have ever done, and he is not ashamed of you. He loves you so much that he died on the cross for your sins. There is no greater love than this.

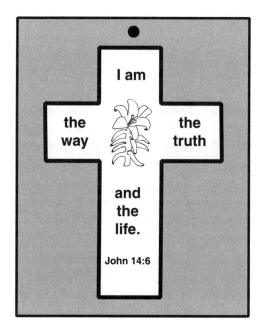

What To Do

1. Cut out the Cross Template.
2. Trace the Cross Template onto the center of card stock.
3. Fold the card stock in half to cut out the cross shape without cutting the border.
4. Glue a clear plastic transparency sheet to the back of the card stock.
5. With a black permanent marker, trace one lily pattern onto the transparency sheet in the center of the cross.
6. Color the leaves and stamen with colored permanent markers.
7. Write the memory verse on the four extensions of the cross (see sketch).
8. Punch a hole in the top of the frame for hanging.
9. Take a suction cup hook home and hang your sun catcher in a window.

Cross Template

New Life

Christ has been raised from the dead. He is the first of a great harvest of all who have died. **1 Corinthians 15:20**

What You Need

- Bibles • Several different types of seeds • Bowls • Resealable plastic bags, one for each child • Permanent markers

Preparation

Place seeds in various bowls on the table where children can reach.

What It's All About

In West Africa, families plant seeds on Good Friday as they think of Jesus' sacrifice. They wait for the resurrection of the plants as they think about the resurrection of Jesus. Today we'll get to celebrate the way they do in West Africa.

What To Do

1. Read the following verses aloud:
   - 1 Corinthians 15:20–22
   - 1 Corinthians 15:35–38
   - 1 Corinthians 15:42–44
   - 1 Corinthians 15:50
   - 1 Corinthians 15:53–58
2. With permanent marker, write one verse or verse reference on a resealable bag.
3. Put a handful of seeds in your resealable plastic bag.
4. Color the picture of the sprout as a reminder to care for your plants when you get home.
5. When you get home, plant the seeds in potting soil and add a little water. Put them near a window and watch to see what grows!

Sign on the Cross

[Jesus] humbled himself in obedience to God and died a criminal's death on a cross. **Philippians 2:8**

What You Need
- Bible • Crayons or markers

Preparation
Photocopy this page, making one for each child.

What It's All About
On Good Friday, we remember that Jesus died for our sins. When Jesus was crucified on the cross, Roman soldiers put a sign above him to mock him. They did not realize that Jesus was showing the power of his love by dying for sinners.

What To Do
Decode the mysterious writing to find out what was on the sign on Jesus' cross. Hint: A-B-C = 1-2-3. Then, look up John 19:19 to check your answer.

___ ___ ___ ___ ___
10   5   19   21   19

of Nazareth

___ ___ ___ ___
11   9   14   7

___ ___
15   6

___ ___ ___
20   8   5

___ ___ ___ ___
10   5   23   19

Good Friday • 47

Jesus Died So We Can Live

He personally carried our sins in his body on the cross so that we can be dead to sin and live for what is right. By his wounds you are healed. **1 Peter 2:24**

What It's All About

When God sent Jesus to be our Savior, he came as a baby. His mission was to grow up, die for us on a cross, and then rise from the dead. It was all part of God's plan to correct the problem of human sin that began in the Garden of Eden. God's plan has always been to save us from the punishment for our sin. Jesus was born to die so that we can have eternal life.

Color the picture.

A God of Promises

Not a single one of all the good promises the LORD had given to the family of Israel was left unfulfilled; everything he had spoken came true. **Joshua 21:45**

What It's All About

Our God is a God of promises. He has always been faithful to keep his promises to us. The rainbow is a reminder that God promised to never again flood the earth. When God promised the world a Savior, he kept that promise through his Son, Jesus. He has promised us that Jesus will return.

Color the picture as a reminder of God's promises.

Good Friday • 49

© 2021 Rose Publishing, LLC. Permission to photocopy granted to original purchaser only. *The Super-Sized Book of Holidays, Special Days, & Celebrations.*

Jesus Is Not Ashamed of Us

Never be ashamed to tell others about our Lord. **2 Timothy 1:8**

What It's All About

Sometimes we get afraid of what others might think of us if they find out we go to church. But Jesus is not ashamed of us, so we should not be afraid and ashamed of him.

Write why you are not ashamed of Jesus on the lines in the cross. Then, color Jesus.

Jesus on the Cross

The message of the cross is foolish to those who are headed for destruction! But we who are being saved know it is the very power of God. **1 Corinthians 1:18**

What It's All About

Crucifixion was cruel. Death was slow and painful, sometimes lasting several days. Jesus was beaten and then made to carry his own cross until he was too weak to carry it any farther. Once outside Jerusalem, at Golgotha, he was nailed to the cross. For three hours, darkness filled the sky even though it was the middle of the day.

Draw the dark clouds in the sky, and then color the picture.

Good Friday • 51

Easter Story Object Lesson

Go quickly and tell his disciples that he has risen from the dead. **Matthew 28:7**

What You Need
- Easter Story Objects (p. 53) • Scissors • 12 plastic, fillable Easter eggs

Preparation
Photocopy Easter Story Objects. Cut the pictures along the lines. Hide one picture inside of each egg. Hide the eggs around the room for children to find. If you have a large class, print multiple copies and hide multiple sets of eggs.

What It's All About
Easter Sunday celebrates the most important event in history—Jesus' death and resurrection. Today, we're going to play a game to tell the story of Easter.

What You Do
After children have found all the eggs, gather together. Children open their eggs. Go down the list asking children to hold up each picture one at a time. Children tell what the item represents and how it's related to the Easter story.

1. **Donkey:** reminds us of Jesus' triumphal entry into Jerusalem.
2. **Bag of coins:** Judas was paid with coins to betray Jesus.
3. **Rooster:** Peter denied Jesus three times before the rooster crowed.
4. **Rope:** Soldiers bound Jesus' hands and led him away.
5. **Crown of thorns:** Placed on Jesus' head to mock him.
6. **Cross:** Jesus carried his own cross to Calvary.
7. **Sponge:** Soldiers offered Jesus vinegar to drink.
8. **Stones:** the rocks split and the earth quaked when Jesus died.
9. **Soldier's helmet:** the centurion said, "Truly this is the Son of God."
10. **Piece of white linen:** Nicodemus and Joseph took Jesus' body down from the cross and placed it in the tomb.
11. **Angel wings:** the angel said, "He is not here, he is risen."
12. **Cloud:** Jesus went to live with his Father in Heaven.

Alternate Idea
Before class, collect objects to represent each of the twelve items in the "What You Do" list. Hide the items around the room. When class starts, have children search for the items. When all items are found, gather the children and discuss how each item relates to the Easter story.

Easter Story Objects

Easter • 53

Easter Newspaper

Go into all the world and preach the Good News to everyone. **Mark 16:15**

What You Need

- Crayons or markers • Paper

Preparation

At least two weeks before Maundy Thursday (the day before Good Friday), photocopy this page, making one for each child.

What to Do

1. Children write an article, poem, song, or story or draw a picture about the Easter story.
2. Collect each child's paper at the end of class. Assemble papers together to make a newspaper. Make enough copies for each child.
3. Hand out the assembled newspapers on Good Friday, or on Easter Sunday.

Alternate Idea

After collecting the children's papers, lay it out in newspaper format. Contact a printer who will print your edition on regular newsprint and fold it like a newspaper or have it copied onto 11x17-inch paper and folded in half. Be sure you have enough copies printed so that there will be one for each home in the area surrounding your church and have extras to give out at special services. Ask volunteers to deliver the papers to homes in your church neighborhood.

Title

Subtitle

Author

_____

_____

_____

_____

_____

_____

Image

Caption

_____

_____

_____

Easter Lilies Crossword

Look at the lilies and how they grow. They don't work or make their clothing, yet Solomon in all his glory was not dressed as beautifully as they are. **Luke 12:27**

What You Need
- Crayons or markers

Preparation
Photocopy this page, making one for each child.

What It's All About
The EASTER LILY reminds us of Easter for many REASONS. First, it's WHITE color reminds us of Jesus' PURITY. He never SINNED, but through his DEATH he WASHED away all our SINS. Second, the trumpet shape of the FLOWER reminds us of the JOYFUL NEWS of Jesus's RESURRECTION.

In Bible times, when there was news, a MESSENGER would blow a TRUMPET or a ram's HORN. Lastly, the flowers turn DOWNWARD to remind us to BOW down and WORSHIP JESUS.

What To Do
1. Fit the capitalized words from the Easter Lilies story into the crossword. Start by counting the letters in each word.
2. Enter the longest and shortest words into the crossword. Then, fill in the rest.

Easter A-Cross-Tic

The Son of Man must be betrayed into the hands of sinful men and be crucified, [so] that he would rise again on the third day. **Luke 24:7**

What You Need
- Crayons or markers

Preparation
Photocopy this page, making one for each child. Optional: Write the activity on a white board and make it a group activity.

What It's All About
Easter is the time of year that we remember Jesus's sacrifice on the cross. He died to free us of our sins, but he didn't stay dead. Three days later he rose from the dead. That's worth celebrating!

What To Do
Based on the Easter story, for each sentence, write the correct word to fill in the blanks.

E for the ___ ___ ___ ___ ___ tomb on that morning. (Rhymes with *tempt me*.)

A for the ___ ___ ___ ___ ___ who greeted the women.

S for the ___ ___ ___ ___ ___ that rolled away.

T for the ___ ___ ___ ___ that could not contain our Lord.

E for ___ ___ ___ ___ ___ ___, the Sunday we celebrate.

R for the ___ ___ ___ ___ ___ ___ ___ ___ who saves us from sin.

Easter A-Cross-Tic: (E) empty (A) angel (S) stone (T) tomb (E) Easter (R) Redeemer.

Resurrection A-Cross-Tic

Then the angel spoke to the women. "Don't be afraid!" he said. "I know you are looking for Jesus, who was crucified." **Matthew 28:5**

Preparation
Photocopy this page, making one for each child. Optional: Write the activity on a white board and make it a group activity.

What It's All About
I'm going to read an Easter Story and emphasize certain words.

"CRUCIFY him!" cried Jesus' enemies at his TRIAL. PILATE, the judge, finally agreed. They nailed Jesus to a CROSS. On the CROSS, Jesus DIED for the sins of the whole world. He was BURIED in a TOMB. A STONE covered the entrance, and SOLDIERS stood outside as guards. On the first day of the week, women came to put SPICES on Jesus' body. They saw an ANGEL, who said, "Jesus is not here; He is RISEN!"

What To Do
Based on the capitalized words in the Easter story, write the correct word to fill in the blanks. Tip: Count the number of letters in each capitalized word, and the number of blanks in each line.

Resurrection A-Cross-Tic: (R) crucify (E) spices (S) stone (U) buried (R) risen (R) trial (E) died (C) cross (T) tomb (I) Pilate (O) soldiers (N) angel.

Our Easter Traditions

God released [Jesus] from the horrors of death and raised him back to life, for death could not keep him in its grip. Acts 2:24

What It's All About

Our Easter traditions go back to a time when a tribe of people held yearly spring feasts. These people worshiped the springtime because of the new life that appeared in the plants after a long and cold winter. But after they heard about Jesus' resurrection, the people changed their feast to celebrate his resurrection. The symbols for their feast were the rabbit and the egg, which represented new life. Out of this came our customs of the Easter Bunny and Easter eggs.

Color the picture.

58 • Easter

The Sunrise and the Risen Son

Christ died for our sins, just as the Scriptures said. He was buried, and he was raised from the dead on the third day, just as the Scriptures said. **1 Corinthians 15:3–4**

What It's All About

Years ago, when the people held their spring feasts, they were celebrating the new life that appeared in the plants in springtime. They were also celebrating the season of the rising sun, or the dawn, and worshiping the sun. Dawn is the early part of the day when the sun rises. Today when Christians celebrate Easter, we celebrate the risen Son, Jesus Christ, by honoring and worshiping him.

Draw sun rays behind Jesus and color the picture. Keep this as a reminder that Jesus is God's risen Son.

Symbols of Easter

Through Christ you have come to trust in God. And you have placed your faith and hope in God because he raised Christ from the dead and gave him great glory. **1 Peter 1:21**

What It's All About

Sometimes, we receive gifts or treats for Easter. Gifts are fun, but they're not what Easter is all about! Easter is about celebrating Jesus's resurrection, the best gift we can ever receive. The resurrection of our Lord and Savior is the greatest of all of the celebrations that Christians observe. Our faith and hope rest in this important event in history. Had Jesus not risen from the dead, we would have no hope of eternal life. Thanks be to God for the grace he gave us in the resurrection of our Lord!

Color the pictures below as a reminder that Jesus' death and resurrection is the center of our Easter celebrations.

Jesus Is Risen

For it is my Father's will that all who see his Son and believe in him should have eternal life. I will raise them up at the last day. **John 6:40**

What It's All About

Jesus overpowered death by becoming alive again! We celebrate Easter because Jesus' tomb was empty. He is risen! The huge stone that was placed over the tomb's doorway was rolled.

Draw the huge stone that was rolled away to reveal an empty tomb. Then, add the women who discovered Jesus' empty tomb and the angel who told them Jesus wasn't there. Color the rest of the picture.

Easter • 61

© 2021 Rose Publishing, LLC. Permission to photocopy granted to original purchaser only. *The Super-Sized Book of Holidays, Special Days, & Celebrations.*

Colors of Easter

All praise to God, the Father of our Lord Jesus Christ. It is by his great mercy that we have been born again, because God raised Jesus Christ from the dead. **1 Peter 1:3**

What It's All About

Easter eggs are fun to paint with brightly colored dyes. The different colors symbolize the various aspects of the Easter story. Red stands for the blood of Jesus and his death. Purple symbolizes the hours of sorrow and pain that Jesus endured during the crucifixion. Black stands for the sin in our lives. White is for the grace of God and how he cleanses us and makes us pure. Pink is symbolic of the hope that we have in him and our new life.

Color each circle on the palette one of the colors: red, purple, black, white, or pink. Then decorate the two eggs using these colors.

He Makes All Things New

Anyone who belongs to Christ has become a new person. The old life is gone; a new life has begun! **2 Corinthians 5:17**

What It's All About

Do you know how a butterfly develops from a cocoon? It grows and grows in the cocoon until finally it emerges as a beautiful butterfly. The butterfly is not the same creature it was when it was in the cocoon. When you become a Christian, you are like a butterfly. You might look the same on the outside, but your heart is changed because you are living for Jesus. People won't notice any difference in your looks, but they will notice the difference in your behavior.

Draw wings on the butterfly and a tulip on the empty stem. Then color the rest of the picture.

Victory Over Death

For this is how God loved the world: He gave his one and only Son, so that everyone who believes in him will not perish but have eternal life. **John 3:16**

What You Need
- Easter Greeting (p. 65)
- Crayons or markers

Preparation
Photocopy this page and Easter Greeting, making one of each page for each child.

What It's All About
On several occasions, Jesus told his disciples and friends that he would rise from the dead, but they forgot. The angel at the empty tomb reminded the women that Jesus rose from the dead just as he said he would. Sometimes as we celebrate Easter, we also may need to be reminded of Jesus' triumphant victory over death.

Color the cross. Keep it as a reminder of Jesus' great love and sacrifice. On Easter Greeting, draw flowers at the foot of the cross and a heart in the center of the cross. Color the rest of the picture. Give the page to someone as a reminder of Jesus' resurrection.

Easter Greeting

To: _____

From: _____

Wishing you Easter blessings as you celebrate the resurrection of Jesus Christ, our Lord and Savior.

Jesus Is Lord of All

The angel said, "Don't be alarmed. You are looking for Jesus of Nazareth, who was crucified. He isn't here! He is risen from the dead! **Mark 16:6**

What You Need
- Easter Wish (p. 67) • Crayons or markers

Preparation
Photocopy this page and Easter Wish, making one of each page for each child.

What It's All About
Jesus' name is more powerful than any on Earth. Jesus died, rose from the dead, and saved us from our sins. We should be very happy that Jesus invites us to share in his kingdom. We show him love and adoration for what he has done.

Color the picture below. On the Easter Wish, draw more flowers around the cross and write "He is Risen" on the banner. Color the rest of the picture. Give the Easter Wish to a friend or family member who doesn't know Jesus as the King of kings.

Easter Wish

To: _____

From: _____

May you know our risen Lord as King of kings!
Wishing you a blessed Easter.

Angelic Announcement

I am the resurrection and the life. Anyone who believes in me will live, even after dying. **John 11:25**

What You Need
- Angel Announcement (p. 69) • Crayons or markers

Preparation
Photocopy this page and Angel Announcement, making one of each page for each child.

What It's All About
Angels are God's special messengers. Angels appeared to the shepherds to announce Jesus' birth. And angels announced that Jesus was no longer dead, but alive! What exciting news the angels shared! You can be a special messenger, too, and tell people the good news.

Color the picture below. On Angel Announcement, draw wings on the angel and color the rest of the picture. Can you think of someone to whom you can tell the exciting news of Jesus? Give the Angel Announcement to that person.

68 • Easter

Angel Announcement

To: _____

From: _____

Jesus is alive! He's no longer dead!
May you experience the joy of his resurrection this Easter.

Happy Easter

[Jesus] showed them the wounds in his hands and his side. They were filled with joy when they saw the Lord! **John 20:20**

What You Need
- Easter Joy (p. 71) • Crayons or markers

Preparation
Photocopy this page and Easter Joy, making one of each page for each child.

What It's All About

Does your family color Easter eggs? Do you go to an Easter egg hunt at your church or in your community? Does your church have an early morning sunrise service to celebrate Easter? These are all Easter traditions because many people do them every year. Traditions help us remember why we celebrate. It's all because Jesus died and rose again to save us from our sins. That's why Easter is such a happy occasion!!

Color the picture. Then, decorate the Easter eggs on Easter Joy and give the sheet to someone for Easter.

70 • Easter

© 2021 Rose Publishing, LLC. Permission to photocopy granted to original purchaser only. *The Super-Sized Book of Holidays, Special Days, & Celebrations.*

Easter Joy

To: _____

From: _____

The disciples saw their Lord
And they were no longer sad;
For Jesus the Lord had risen
Which makes us, too, very glad.

As we celebrate Easter, remember it is Jesus who fills us with joy because of his resurrection.

Celebrate Easter

Christ Jesus died for us and was raised to life for us, and he is sitting in the place of honor at God's right hand, pleading for us. **Romans 8:34**

What You Need
- Easter Wreath (p. 73) • Crayons or markers

Preparation
Photocopy this page and Easter Wreath, making one of each page for each child.

What It's All About
When we celebrate Easter, we celebrate the resurrection of Jesus Christ, our Lord. Easter gives us the hope of eternal life through Jesus. You can share what Easter is all about with someone who does not know.

Color this page. Then, on Easter Wreath, draw a picture of Jesus inside the heart wreath or write his name. Give it to someone who needs to know Jesus as their Savior. Color the page and keep it as a reminder of the reason why we celebrate Easter.

Easter Wreath

To: _____

From: _____

This Easter, remember that Jesus gave us life through his death.
Praise God for his grace and love!

Protected by God

For you [God] are my hiding place; you protect me from trouble. You surround me with songs of victory. **Psalm 32:7**

What It's All About

Passover celebrates a time when the Israelites were still slaves in Egypt. The last and final plague that God sent to free his people was the death of every Egyptian family's firstborn son. God provided the Israelites protection from this terrible plague. Through Moses, God commanded the Israelites to paint the blood of a lamb on their doors. When the angel of death went through the land of Egypt, he passed over the homes with blood on the doors.

Color this picture as a reminder that Jesus is the lamb who was sacrificed so that we can have eternal life. The blood of the lamb represented the promise of a future Savior: Jesus. When Jesus came to Earth, he died to save everyone who believes in him.

Stained Glass Window

Christ, our Passover Lamb, has been sacrificed for us. **1 Corinthians 5:7**

What It's All About

For the tenth plague of Egypt, the Israelites had to kill a lamb and paint its blood on their doors so that the angel of death would not visit them. Jesus is like that lamb because he died for us. Our sins have been paid by Jesus, but we must first accept him.

Color the picture. Do you want to be saved by the Lamb's blood? If so, then tell a trusted adult who can help you make this important step.

Passover • 75

© 2021 Rose Publishing, LLC. Permission to photocopy granted to original purchaser only. *The Super-Sized Book of Holidays, Special Days, & Celebrations.*

Stained Glass Church

He isn't here! He is risen from the dead, just as he said would happen. **Matthew 28:6**

What You Need

- Church Template (p. 77) • Scissors • Ruler • White paper
- Pictures of the class, instant camera, or old magazines
- Colored paper scraps or tissue paper
- Glue • Markers • White poster board
- Black construction paper

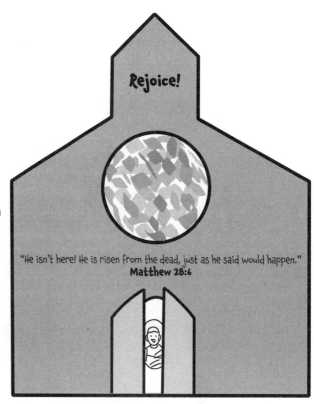

Preparation

Photocopy Church Template, making one set for each child. Cut 3x3-inch paper squares, making one for each child. If pictures of your class are not available, bring an instant camera or provide magazines for the children to cut out pictures.

What It's All About

Pentecost celebrates the day the Holy Spirit descended on the apostles. It is also the beginning of the Church's mission on Earth; to spread the news of the gospel. The Church with a big C is a group of Christians who believe that Jesus died and rose for their sins. The church with a little C is a place where Christians come together to worship God.

The Bible tells us that we need to come together to encourage one another. It is important that we appreciate the church as God's house and treat it with respect and reverence.

The early believers did not have a special place to worship together. But as the numbers of believers grew, church buildings were built. Some of the most beautiful old churches have stained glass windows. These windows brought beautiful light into the sanctuary.

Today, we will make our own stained glass church to celebrate Pentecost.

What To Do

1. Tear colored paper scraps or tissue paper into small pieces.
2. Glue the torn paper on the 3x3-inch piece of paper in a mosaic fashion. Cover the entire area. The scraps can overlap slightly, but try to keep the same colors from touching.
3. Using the pattern, trace and cut a church from white poster board. Fold the church in half to cut out the center circle.
4. Outline the back of the circle hole with glue and place the collage of colors behind it to give it a stained glass window effect. A corner of the paper may need to be trimmed so it doesn't show.
5. Trace the door pattern outline onto the church to use as a guide for gluing on the church doors.
6. Cut a set of doors from black construction paper.
7. Fold the tabs as shown and glue only the tabs to the church so that the doors can swing open.
8. Glue a picture of people inside the church.
9. Outline the building with marker and write the memory verse on the front.

Church Template

Pentecost • 77

Pentecost Celebration

You will receive power when the Holy Spirit comes upon you. And you will be my witnesses, telling people about me everywhere. **Acts 1:8**

What It's All About

The festival of Pentecost is full of excitement. It celebrates the coming of the Holy Spirit. The apostles were in the upper room when a sound like a rushing mighty wind filled the house. Above them appeared tongues of fire that filled them with power to speak other languages. They went into the streets and told the story of Jesus.

Three thousand people believed and became followers of Jesus from this day. What a wonderful time to give praise and thanksgiving for the start of the Christian Church.

What to Do

Have a grand surprise party for the whole family of God. The following are some suggestions for the celebration.

Plan a Parade

- Crayons or markers • Computer and printer (or prepare these ahead of time)
- Scissors • Construction paper • Glue • Poster board
- Red, orange, or yellow balloons • String or ribbon

Make banners! Draw flames (the Holy Spirit), a bunch of grapes (fruit of the Spirit), or write the words *joy, peace,* and *hallelujah*. Children write the words and draw the symbols on construction paper, cut them out, and glue them to the poster board sheet(s).

Use red, orange, and yellow balloons to symbolize the tongues of fire over the apostles' heads. Fill balloons with helium and tether with strings or ribbon in matching colors. Tie a balloon to each child's wrist.

Children march around the church, singing songs of praise, with their balloons and banners.

Fruit of the Spirit Snack

- Hand wipes • Fruit • Paper plates

Children clean hands with wipes, and then choose fruit to place on a paper plate. As they eat, teacher says, The Holy Spirit is known for twelve gifts called the fruit of the Spirit. When you invite the Holy Spirit into your life, your mindset and attitude will start to change. These changes are called fruit. The fruit of the Spirit are love, joy, peace, patience, kindness, goodness, faithfulness, gentleness, and self-control.

Invite Others

- Paper • Crayons or markers • Pins • Red yarn or ribbon

Invite family members and other congregation members to visit your classroom. Make a sign to place on your door saying, "You are now entering your Field of Ministry." Symbolize the Spirit's calling of each one to ministry by pinning a length of red yarn or ribbon on their shoulder.

How to Surprise Others

The Holy Spirit gives gifts to each of God's children. Our children can prepare gifts for others to symbolize this act. Encourage children to make a gift at home during the week and to keep it a surprise until the end of the Pentecost celebration. Then . . . surprise! They give their gifts to people in the congregation: shut-ins, grandparents, and others.

The Fruit of the Holy Spirit

When the Father sends the Advocate as my representative—that is, the Holy Spirit—he will teach you everything and will remind you of everything I have told you. **John 14:26**

What You Need
- Crayons or markers

Preparation
Photocopy this page, making one for each child.

What It's All About
When the Holy Spirit came to Earth on the day of Pentecost, he came to stay. He is always with you, and he helps your faith grow. As a tree grows, it produces fruit. When your faith grows, it produces the fruit of the Spirit. This means that your faith produces good things.

What To Do
Match the fruit in the word box on the right to the action on the left. If some of the fruits sound similar to you, that's OK! Just try to find one example for each of the fruit. Then, circle some of these actions that you can do this week and color the picture.

1. Wait for others to get their food before you.
2. Hug a friend or family member.
3. Invite someone sitting alone to have lunch with you.
4. Sing praises to God.
5. Write a pledge with your friends to not argue or gossip.
6. Give your old toys or clothes to someone in need.
7. Comfort a sad friend.
8. Make a prayer or Bible-reading chart.
9. When you are angry, take five deep breaths before you respond.

Word Box
Love
Joy
Peace
Patience
Kindness
Goodness
Faithfulness
Gentleness
Self-Control

Search for God's Word

Everyone present was filled with the Holy Spirit and began speaking in other languages, as the Holy Spirit gave them this ability. **Acts 2:4**

What You Need
- Crayons or markers

Preparation
Photocopy this page, making one for each child.

What It's All About
Forty days after Jesus rose again, Jesus said to his disciples, "STAY in Jerusalem until the HOLY SPIRIT comes. Then GO and tell all people about ME." The disciples saw Jesus lift up from the earth and go toward Heaven. He was GONE! Then about 120 believers met in a room, where they waited and PRAYED. TEN DAYS went by. On the day of PENTECOST, they heard the SOUND of a violent WIND. What looked like tongues of FIRE SAT on each head. The Holy Spirit filled the believers, and they began to speak in other LANGUAGES. Out in the streets, they PREACHED about Jesus. People from many COUNTRIES could HEAR the GOSPEL in their own language, and about THREE thousand people were SAVED that day.

What To Do
Find and circle the capitalized words from the story in the word search going down, across, and diagonally.

Five-Finger Prayer

We are confident that he hears us whenever we ask for anything that pleases him. **1 John 5:14**

What You Need
- Crayons or markers • Paper

What It's All About
The National Day of Prayer encourages all believers to pray. Jesus stressed the importance of prayer in his teachings as well in his own life. He often went away from the crowds to spend time in prayer. Even in his final days on Earth, he prayed to his Father.

You can pray anytime or anywhere, and God will hear you. It doesn't matter if your prayers are long or short, God just likes to hear from you. Today, we'll do an activity to teach you how to pray.

What To Do
1. Trace your hand on a piece of paper.
2. Write a prayer on each finger in the following order (or write a word that will remind you of the prayer):
   - Thumb: Write a prayer for your family.
   - Pointer: Write a prayer for your school or teachers.
   - Middle: Write a prayer for the country.
   - Ring: Write a prayer for someone in need.
   - Pinky: Write a prayer for yourself.

> An easy way to remember the categories for each finger is to look at your hand. The thumb is closest to you, so you pray for your family. The pointer gives you direction, like your teachers. The middle finger stands above all the others. The ring finger is usually the weakest. The pinky is the smallest.

3. When everyone has written their prayers, gather in a circle and bring your papers.
4. A volunteer will start the prayer by praying out loud or silently about one or two things on their list. The volunteer ends the prayer by saying, "Amen."
5. The volunteer then chooses the next person to pray.
6. Continue until everyone has had a chance to pray.

Prayer Code

Never stop praying. **1 Thessalonians 5:17**

What You Need
- Crayons or markers

Preparation
Photocopy this page, making one for each child.

What It's All About
The National Day of Prayer is a special day that reminds us to pray. God doesn't need us to pray to him. Prayer is our way of worshiping God and reminding ourselves that he is in control. You can pray when you are happy, sad, lonely, or stressed. God will always hear your prayers.

Is this special day of prayer the only time we should pray? Compete this prayer code to find out how often we should pray.

What To Do
Each number under the blanks corresponds to a number on the clock. Write the letter under the clock number on the blanks.

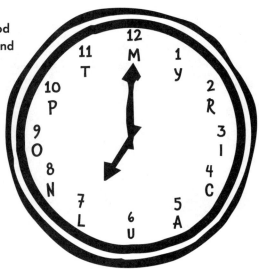

___ ___ ___ ___
10 2   5   1

___ ___ ___ ___ ___ ___ ___ ___ ___ ___ ___
4   9   8   11 3   8   6   5   7   7   1

___ ___ ___ ___ ___ ___ E.
5   8   1   11 3   12

We can't pray every minute of our day, but we can talk to him all through the day, wherever we are. In the space below, write your own prayer to God.

_____

_____

_____

_____

God's Promise to the Israelites

For I command you this day to love the LORD your God and to keep his commands, decrees, and regulations by walking in his ways. **Deuteronomy 30:16**

What It's All About

Shavuot, which means weeks in Hebrew, celebrates when Moses received the Ten Commandments after weeks of traveling. God faithfully brought the Israelites out of Egypt, using Moses as their leader. God promised to give the people a new land with a new way of living.

Shavuot is celebrated at the beginning of the harvest and is sometimes known as the Feast of First Fruits. God told the Israelites that if they obeyed his commands by loving and serving only him, he would bless them with an abundance of crops.

Draw the Ten Commandments in Moses' hands and fruit on the tree. Then color the picture.

Harvest Festival

Blessed are those who trust in the LORD and have made the LORD their hope and confidence. **Jeremiah 17:7**

What It's All About

Shavuot is a harvest festival and a religious festival. It celebrates the giving of the Ten Commandments at the time of the harvest. Many Jews read the story of Ruth during this holiday. Ruth was a foreigner who arrived in Israel during the time of the barley harvest. Because of her faithfulness to God, she became an ancestor of King David. Her story reminds us that anyone who believes in God is welcomed into the family of believers.

Draw yourself and another believer on the blank faces below. Then, color the other faces.

Shout It Out Shofar

Shout to the LORD, all the earth; break out in praise and sing for joy! **Psalm 98:4**

What You Need

- Construction paper or card stock • Ruler
- Scissors • Crayons or markers • Glue

Preparation

Photocopy this page, making one for each child. Cut strips of construction paper or card stock into 1x5-inch strips. Cut at least three for each child.

What It's All About

Rosh Hashanah which means *head of the year,* celebrates the Jewish New Year and the creation of the world. It is a celebration where the Jewish people traditionally eat apples dipped in honey to represent a sweet year ahead. The *shofar* is a trumpet-like instrument made from a ram's horn. It is blown during the Rosh Hashanah service. Shofars can make a beautiful, but loud, noise! They are used to announce or introduce good news. We will use our shofars to shout out our praises to God.

Optional

Offer children apples and honey as a snack after the activity.

What To Do

1. Cut out the shofar.
2. Write the memory verse on the shofar. Then, color the shofar.
3. Glue the shofar onto a piece of card stock or construction paper.
4. Write praises to God or things that you are grateful for onto the pre-cut strips of paper.
5. Glue the praise strips on the paper like they are coming out of the shofar. It's OK if they extend off the card stock or construction paper.

Feast of Tabernacles

Taste and see that the LORD is good. Oh, the joys of those who take refuge in him! **Psalm 34:8**

What It's All About

The Jewish Feast of Tabernacles, also known as *Sukkot*, celebrated the final harvest. Israelites constructed huts made of fresh branches, palm trees, and willows in the streets, courts, public squares, and on roofs. For seven days, families lived in these huts as a reminder of God's fatherly care and protection when he guided them from Egypt to Canaan. Celebrations renewed their faith and taught the children about God's goodness.

Color the picture.

Prayer of Atonement

On that day offerings of purification will be made for you, and you will be purified in the LORD's presence from all your sins. **Leviticus 16:30**

What It's All About

Yom Kippur means *day of atonement* and many Jewish people consider it the holiest day of the year. Atonement means to make something right that was done wrong. On this day, Jews ask for forgiveness from God and from family or friends for any sins that they committed during the year. They focus on prayer by not eating, drinking, or working.

Write your own prayer in the word bubble below. If you run out of room, continue on the bed spread. Then, color the praying child to look like you, and color the rest of the picture.

Yom Kippur • 87

Reformation Day Celebration

God saved you by his grace when you believed. And you can't take credit for this; it is a gift from God. **Ephesians 2:8**

What It's All About

In the Middle Ages, most people did not know how to read. They relied on priests to tell them Bible stories. After the printing press was invented, Bibles were distributed for people to read on their own. Martin Luther was a monk who began to read his Bible on his own. He believed other people should be able to read the Bible for themselves, too.

Martin Luther discovered that the Catholic church was not obeying many biblical rules. He wrote out ninety-five problems on a document called the *Ninety-Five Theses*. Luther nailed his list to his church door on October 31, 1517. Historians consider this the start of the Protestant Reformation. Today, many people celebrate Reformation Day on October 31 in honor of Luther's work.

Departing the Dark Ages

Send out invitations inviting children to depart from the Dark Ages and enter the Reformation Era. Include the date, time, and party place, and advise children to dress in Renaissance attire. Some examples might be a monk, nun, knight, maiden, or member of royalty. Provide masks for anyone arriving without a costume. See Queen Mask and King Mask on pages 35–36.

Stamps Station

- Letter stamps • Ink pads • Paper

The printing press was hugely important in spreading the news of the Reformation. Organize a table with stamp letters for children to write messages.

Sing Songs Written by Martin Luther

Search online for the lyrics to the following songs written by Martin Luther and sing them as a group.

- "A Mighty Fortress Is Our God"
- "Out of the Depth I Cry to Thee"
- "Dearest Jesus"
- "Away in a Manger"
- "Savior of the Nations, Come"

For a Reformation object lesson or coloring page, see Luther's Rose on page 89.

Reformation Snacks

Choose a snack for your party or enjoy both! Include a short note beside the snack for context.

Hammer Snack

- Pretzels • Marshmallows
- Chocolate spread • Plate or bowl

Luther's hammering of the *Ninety-Five Theses* was heard around the world. It began the Protestant revolution.

What to Do

1. Press a pretzel stick into a marshmallow to make it look like a hammer.
2. Spread chocolate spread on one end of the marshmallow.
3. Place on a plate or in a bowl.

Diet of Worms

- Chocolate pudding cups • Plastic spoons
- Crushed chocolate sandwich cookies • Gummy worms

When the Catholic Church read Martin Luther's *Ninety-Five Theses*, they put him on trial before a diet (group of church leaders) in the town of Worms, Germany. Why not snack on a yummy cup of dirt pudding?

What to Do

1. Remove lid from pudding cup and spoon crushed chocolate sandwich cookies on top.
2. Top with gummy worms.
3. Children eat with a plastic spoon.

Luther's Rose

Three things will last forever—faith, hope, and love—and the greatest of these is love. **1 Corinthians 13:13**

What You Need
- Black, red, green, blue, and gold (or yellow) crayons or markers

Preparation
Photocopy this page, making one for each child. Make a finished product to reference while telling the object lesson.

What It's All About
When Martin Luther started the Reformed Church, he designed a symbol called Luther's Rose. It represents a summary of the gospel. Let's start in the center. The black cross represents that Jesus died for us. The cross is in the center of a red believer's heart. If you believe in Jesus with your heart, you will be given eternal life.

The white flower with green leaves around the heart represents your faith, which grows as you dedicate yourself to Jesus. The sky-blue background represents the joy we will have in Heaven. The ring is gold because it is the most valuable metal. But most importantly, the ring has no end because our God eternally surrounds us.

What To Do
Color the cross black, the heart red, the leaves green, the space behind the flower blue, and the outer ring gold or yellow.

Reformation Day • 89

Turkey Tom

I will praise God's name with singing, and I will honor him with thanksgiving. **Psalm 69:30**

What It's All About

There once was a proud turkey named Tom who strutted around the barnyard. Now, Tom was a beautiful turkey with many colorful tail feathers, but he was never happy about anything. He gobble-grumbled about his food, he gobble-grumbled about the place he had to sleep, he even gobble-grumbled about the other animals with whom he had to share the barnyard.

One day, the farmer heard Tom gobble-grumbling about something and he said, "I wish that every time you gobble-grumble about something one of your tail feathers would fall out!" The next day when the farmer came to feed old Tom, he saw an awful sight. Poor old grumbling Tom had lost all his tail feathers! He had gobble-grumbled away all his beauty.

This is just a silly story, but it does have a lesson. People who grumble about everything are not very beautiful, either. Other people don't enjoy being around grumblers. When we complain about what God has given us, we are sinning.

Remember old Tom the next time you are tempted to grumble. Be a beautiful, thankful Christian instead. Answer the questions below, then color the turkey.

Discussion Questions

1. What did grumbling do for Tom?

   _____

   _____

2. How do grumbling people look?

   _____

   _____

3. Name some things for which you are thankful.

   _____

   _____

A Grand Old Gobbler

Enter his gates with thanksgiving; go into his courts with praise. Give thanks to him and praise his name. **Psalm 100:4**

What You Need
- Turkey Template (p. 92) • Card stock • Crayons or markers • Scissors
- Orange, yellow, red, and brown construction paper • Glue • Tape

Preparation
Photocopy this page and Turkey Template onto card stock, making one of each page for each child. Provide a 9x3-inch rectangle of orange paper and a 6x3-inch rectangle of yellow paper for each child.

What It's All About
On Thanksgiving, many families gather together around a turkey dinner and share what they are thankful for. Today, we get to make our own paper turkey. Keep it as a reminder to give God thanks every day.

What To Do
1. Trace and cut one large set of tail feathers from red paper and one small set of tail feathers from yellow construction paper.
2. Glue the feathers together with the yellow on top of the red.
3. Write the memory verse at the top of the yellow feathers.
4. Roll the orange rectangle into a cylinder and tape it closed. This is the turkey body.
5. Glue the cylinder to the bottom center of the yellow feathers.
6. Roll the yellow rectangle into another cylinder and tape it closed. This is the turkey head.
7. Glue this cylinder to the orange cylinder, offsetting the yellow one by about one inch at the top.
8. Use the patterns to trace and cut out two brown wings, one orange beak, and one red wattle from construction paper.
9. Glue one wing to each side of the orange cylinder and the beak and wattle to the front center of the yellow cylinder.
10. Draw two black circles for eyes on each side of the head. Optional: Glue on wiggly eyes.

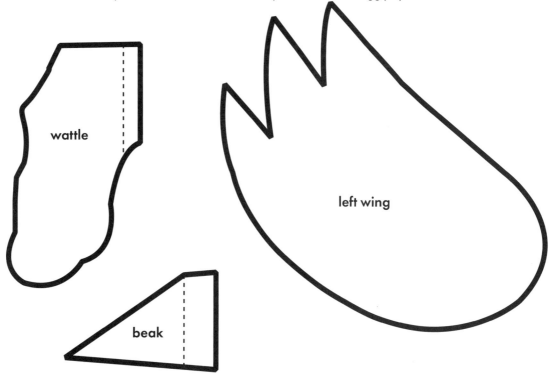

Thanksgiving

Turkey Template

92 • Thanksgiving

Hanging Horn of Plenty

God will generously provide all you need. Then you will always have everything you need and plenty left over to share with others. **2 Corinthians 9:8**

What You Need

- Cornucopia Pattern and Fruit Patterns (pp. 94–95) • Cardstock • Scissors • Ruler • Thread
- Orange construction paper • Poster board • Glue • Crayons or markers • Hole punch

Preparation

Photocopy Cornucopia Pattern and Fruit Patterns onto card stock, making one for each child. Cut four 7-inch lengths of thread for each child.

What It's All About

Pilgrims came to America from England in 1620 seeking religious freedom. Their first winter was very hard, but they survived and learned how to farm. Their second harvest was bountiful, and by decree of Governor William Bradford, the pilgrims held a festival of Thanksgiving in 1621.

Friendly Native Americans helped the pilgrims. Their feasting, praying, singing, and playing lasted for three days.

Today we are going to make a cornucopia, which is a horn-shaped basket often filled with fruit. It is a symbol of having many blessings. At Thanksgiving time, we give thanks for the fullness of our lives and the blessings we receive from God.

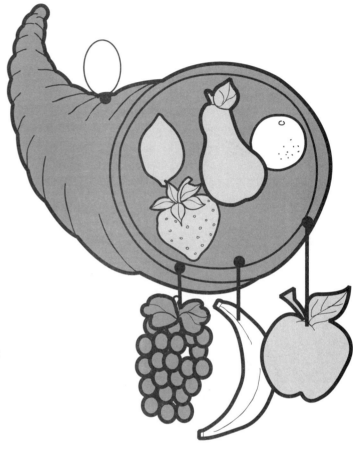

What To Do

1. Trace and cut one cornucopia from orange construction paper and one from poster board. Glue them together.
2. Use a black marker to outline the cornucopia and fill in the markings as indicated on the pattern.
3. Color and cut out the fruit.
4. Glue the lemon, orange, strawberry, and pear to the inside of the cornucopia.
5. Tape a length of thread to the backs of the grapes, banana, and apple.
6. Punch three holes along the bottom rim of the cornucopia and one at top.
7. Tie the fruit through the three bottom holes.
8. Tie a loop at the top of the cornucopia for a hanger.
9. Write the memory verse on the horn of the cornucopia.

Cornucopia Pattern

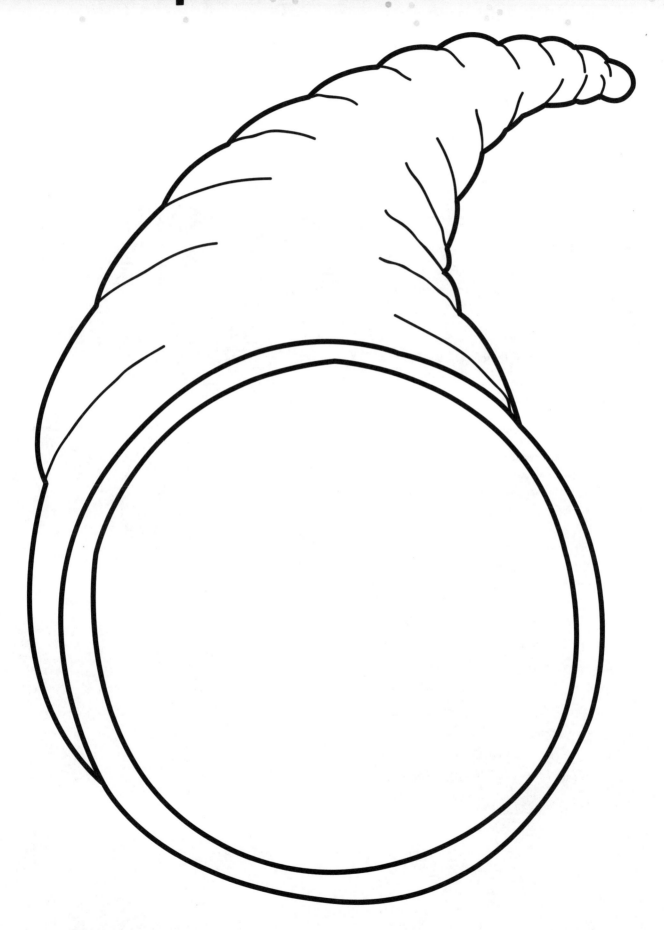

94 • Thanksgiving

Fruit Patterns

Thanksgiving • 95

Thanksgiving Hand Card

Give thanks to the LORD, for he is good! His faithful love endures forever. **Psalm 136:1**

What You Need
- Paper • Crayons or markers

What It's All About
Thanksgiving is a time when we thank God for the blessings he has given us. We can praise God for our friends, family, teachers, country, and more. Today, let's make a turkey card for the people we're thankful for.

Bonus Idea
Make cards for the sick and elderly.

What To Do
1. Fold paper in half to make a card.
2. Trace your hand on the front side of the card.
3. Your thumb will be your turkey's head. Draw a black dot in the center of the thumb for an eye. Optional: Glue on a wiggle eye.
4. Draw a triangle off the tip of the thumb for the beak. Color it yellow.
5. Draw a small upside-down heart shape or a circle shape under the beak for the wattle. Color it red.
6. Draw a wing in the palm of the hand.
7. Draw two legs at the heel of the hand.
8. The other four fingers are the feathers. Color one red, one yellow, one orange, and one brown.
9. Color the rest of the turkey brown.
10. Inside the card, write "I'm so thankful for you!" Add the memory verse if there is room inside. Or write it on the back of the card.
11. Sign your name and give the card to someone you love.
12. Make more cards as time allows.

Thanksgiving Celebration

I will rejoice in the LORD. I will be glad because he rescues me. **Psalm 35:9**

What It's All About
Thanksgiving is a time to let your family and friends know just how much you love them. Let's throw a party to show our attitude of gratitude.

What to Do
Have a grand Thanksgiving party for the whole family of God. The following are some suggestions for the celebration.

Turkey Shoot Game
- Small paper bags • Rubber bands

Blow up small paper bags and close them with rubber bands to make turkeys. Hide turkeys around a room or outside area. Send players to search for the turkeys. When a turkey is found, player pops it. The player who finds the most turkeys recites, or chooses someone to recite the memory verse. Optional: If playing outside, add candy to the bag so it doesn't blow away. Players keep the candy in any turkey they find.

Turkey Leg Wrap Game
- Timer • Burlap or brown wrapping paper • Chef's hat, one for each team of two or three

Players divide into teams of two or three. One volunteer in each group becomes the turkey leg. Set the timer for two minutes. When the timer starts, the partners wrap the volunteer in burlap or brown wrapping paper. After wrapping the volunteer turkey leg, teams place a chef's hat on the volunteer's head. The first team to finish may recite, or choose someone else to recite the memory verse.

Turkey Treats
- Chocolate sandwich cookies • Malted milk balls
- Candy corn • Small cinnamon candies • Plastic knives
- Chocolate frosting • Paper plates

Participants will enjoy making these for themselves. Or make them ahead of time if that works better for your schedule.

For each Turkey Treat: open the cookie and dab a small amount of frosting in the center of one cookie half. Place the malted milk ball on the frosting. Dab chocolate frosting on top of the milk ball and place a cinnamon candy on it.

Spread chocolate frosting in the center of the remaining cookie half and make an arc of frosting above the center. Place five or six candy corns in the arc as turkey feathers. Attach the cookie to the back of the milk ball, so the feathers frame the milk ball, to complete the turkey.

Provide additional cookies and candy for snacking. If time allows, children can make two turkeys so they can eat one and take one home. Talk about God's blessings as the children work.

Thankful Pennant Bunting
- Scissors • Card stock • Crayons or markers • Tape • String

Cut out triangles of identical size. Distribute one to each child. Participants draw what they are thankful for and write their names on the back. Tape the decorated triangles onto the string. Hang it in a visible place for decoration.

Thanksgiving Crossword

Give thanks for everything to God the Father in the name of our Lord Jesus Christ. **Ephesians 5:20**

What You Need
- Crayons or markers

Preparation
Photocopy this page, making one for each child.

What It's All About
At the first Thanksgiving, the pilgrims thanked God for getting them through a terrible winter and blessing them with a wonderful harvest. Take time to thank God for all the blessings he has given you this year.

What To Do
Put the words in the word box into the crossword. Hint: Count how many letters are in each word. Start by putting the longest words in first.

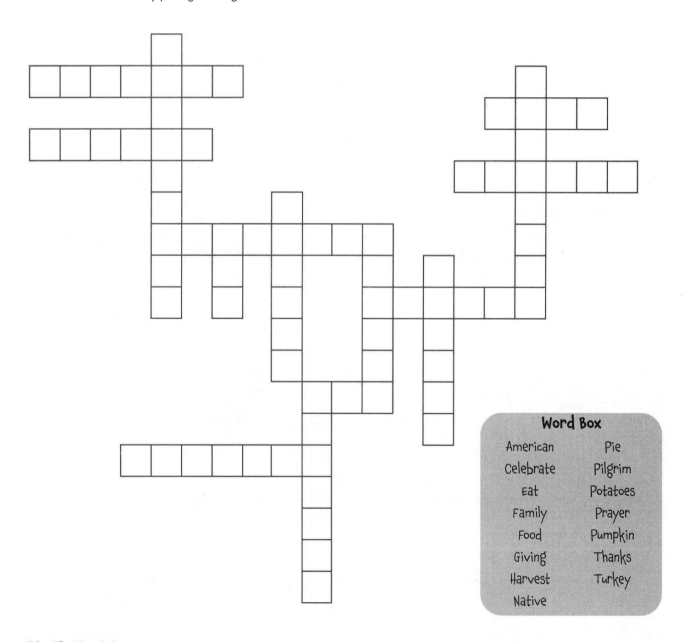

Word Box

American	Pie
Celebrate	Pilgrim
Eat	Potatoes
Family	Prayer
Food	Pumpkin
Giving	Thanks
Harvest	Turkey
Native	

Thanksgiving Code

Let us come to him with thanksgiving. Let us sing psalms of praise to him. **Psalm 95:2**

What You Need
- Crayons or markers

Preparation
Photocopy this page, making one for each child.

What It's All About
Thanksgiving is a time when we thank God for the blessings he has given us. The Pilgrims celebrated Thanksgiving at the end of their harvest. In Bible times, people were expected to give the best crops of the harvest to God. This was a reminder that all good things belong to God, but he loves to share them with us!

If God asked you to give him a gift, would you give it? How often? Use the code to find one special gift God wants from his children.

What To Do
Complete the code according to the key.

Key

A	C	E	F	I	L	N	O	P	R	S	T	U	Y
1	2	3	4	5	6	7	8	9	10	11	12	13	14

The Israelites gave God the first sheaves of wheat from their harvest, called the

___ ___ ___ ___ ___ ___ ___ ___ ___ ___ ___ .
 4   5 10 11 12   4 10 13   5 12 11

Our special gift to God is found in Hebrews 13:15: "Let us offer through Jesus a

___ ___ ___ ___ ___ ___ ___ ___ ___
 2   8   7 12   5   7 13   1   6

___ ___ ___ ___ ___ ___ ___ ___ ___ of
11   1   2 10   5   4   5   2   3

___ ___ ___ ___ ___ ___ to God, proclaiming
 9 10   1   5 11   3

___ ___ ___ allegiance to his name."
 8 13 10

Abundant Blessings

I will bless this city and make it prosperous; I will satisfy its poor with food. **Psalm 132:15**

What You Need
- Crayons or markers

Preparation
Photocopy this page, making one for each child.

What It's All About
At this time of year, many farmers bring the last of their crops into their barns. People harvest the rest of the vegetables from the gardens, and the orchards are full of ripe fruit waiting to be picked.

The Pilgrims were very thankful for the food they had to eat on the first Thanksgiving. They had some very difficult times. They learned to plant and hunt so that they could provide food for their families. They realized what a wonderful blessing God had given them and they wanted to thank him.

Sometimes we forget to be thankful for the abundant blessings we have. God has promised to continue to bless us if we honor him.

Discussion Questions

1. What does *abundance* mean?

   _____

   _____

2. For what were the pilgrims thankful?

   _____

   _____

3. What do we need to do to receive God's blessing?

   _____

   _____

4. Name or draw some of the blessings God has given you, and then thank him for them.

Color Me Turkey
For Younger Elementary Kids

Let us come to him with thanksgiving. Let us sing psalms of praise to him. **Psalm 95:2**

What It's All About
The traditional Thanksgiving turkey meal reminds us of the first American Thanksgiving. Wild turkeys can fly and like to sleep in trees. Plus, their heads can change colors from red to blue to white depending on how excited or calm they are.

What To Do
Color the turkey below according to this color code:

1 = Brown 2 = Orange 3 = Yellow 4 = Red

See page 102 for a color-code activity appropriate for older elementary children.

Thanksgiving • 101

Color Me Turkey
For Older Elementary Kids

Let us come to him with thanksgiving. Let us sing psalms of praise to him. **Psalm 95:2**

What It's All About

Turkeys get their name from the *turk turk* sound that they make when they are scared. They are the most famous symbol for the Thanksgiving holiday because of the first Thanksgiving meal. Tradition says that four wild turkeys were served as a peaceful meal between the Pilgrims and the Native Americans.

> See page 101 for a color-code activity appropriate for younger elementary children.

What To Do

Follow the number guide to color in the picture.

1 - light blue   2 - gray   3 - green   4 - dark green   5 - yellow
6 - orange   7 - red   8 - brown   9 - pink   10 - black

The Pilgrims

For the LORD *your God is bringing you into a good land of flowing streams and pools of water, with fountains and springs that gush out in the valleys and hills.* **Deuteronomy 8:7**

What It's All About

The Pilgrims in Colonial America were Christians committed to Jesus and to the Bible. They believed their voyage from England was like the Hebrews' forty-year wandering in the desert. Here in America they could worship freely and bring the light and hope of Jesus to this land.

Color the picture.

A Thanksgiving Feast

Give thanks to the LORD and proclaim his greatness. Let the whole world know what he has done. **Psalm 105:1**

What It's All About

As they began a new life in America, the Pilgrims endured great trials and hardships. Filled with gratitude for God's divine protection and care, they created a holiday called Thanksgiving. The first Thanksgiving was a joyous occasion for both the Pilgrims and the Native Americans. They had plenty of meat, vegetables, and other good things to eat as well as games to play.

Draw food on the table, then color the picture.

We Celebrate Thanksgiving

Blessing and glory and wisdom and thanksgiving and honor and power and strength belong to our God forever and ever! Amen. **Revelation 7:12**

What It's All About

Thanksgiving Day is the perfect time to remember the blessings God has given us. Although the football games, colorful parades, or delicious turkey dinners are fun, we need to remember who deserves the ultimate thanks. We can thank God every day of the year, not just on special days like Thanksgiving.

Draw Thanksgiving food on the table, then color the picture.

Thanksgiving • 105

© 2021 Rose Publishing, LLC. Permission to photocopy granted to original purchaser only. *The Super-Sized Book of Holidays, Special Days, & Celebrations.*

Harvest Time Abundance

You thrill me, LORD, with all you have done for me! I sing for joy because of what you have done. **Psalm 92:4**

What It's All About

During Thanksgiving, we focus our attention on giving God thanks for the blessings he has provided us, especially during the past year. But we should really thank him every day for even the simple things. We also should thank the people in our lives, such as parents, grandparents, friends, teachers, and church leaders, for the simple things that they do for us. It can change your attitude when you are thankful for even the small things, such as the leaves turning colors and falling from trees.

Draw pumpkins under the tree, make the tree leaves colorful, and color the rest of the picture.

Happy Thanksgiving

The LORD is my strength and shield. I trust him with all my heart. He helps me, and my heart is filled with joy. I burst out in songs of thanksgiving. **Psalm 28:7**

What You Need

- Thanksgiving Blessings (p. 108) • Crayons or markers

Preparation

Photocopy this page and Thanksgiving Blessings, making one for each child.

What It's All About

Thanksgiving is the time of year when we thank God for his many blessings. What's something that someone gave you that you are especially thankful for? This would be a great time to thank someone with a card or note. Color the picture below and keep it as a reminder to be thankful to God for his many blessings.

Draw something you're thankful for inside the pumpkin on the Thanksgiving Blessings page, color it, and give it to someone you want to have a happy Thanksgiving.

Thanksgiving Blessings

To: _____

From: _____

When I count my many blessings
Coming down from God above,
I thank Him for the kindness
You've showed to me in love.
Wishing you a Thanksgiving full of God's blessings!

Thanksgiving Care

The LORD pours down his blessings. Our land will yield its bountiful harvest. **Psalm 85:12**

What You Need
- Thanksgiving Cheer (p. 110) • Crayons or markers

Preparation
Photocopy this page and Thanksgiving Cheer, making one for each child.

What It's All About
Do you know people who could use a little cheering up during Thanksgiving? Holidays are not always happy and joyous times for everyone. But you can make it brighter for others by letting them know you care about them.

Color the picture below. On the Thanksgiving Cheer page, draw more fruit in the basket, color the rest of the picture, and give the sheet to someone special.

Thanksgiving • 109

Thanksgiving Cheer

To: _____

From: _____

May God fill your life with his love and his blessings during Thanksgiving and all through the year.

The First Thanksgiving

Give thanks to the LORD and proclaim his greatness. Let the whole world know what he has done. **1 Chronicles 16:8**

What You Need
- Thanksgiving Leaves (p. 112) • Crayons or markers

Preparation
Photocopy this page and Thanksgiving Leaves, making one for each child.

What It's All About
The Pilgrims did not celebrate the first American harvest until the end of 1621. It had been a very difficult year for them, but by God's grace they survived. George Washington first proclaimed November 26, 1789 as a Thanksgiving holiday. In 1941, Congress made the fourth Thursday of November the national holiday we call Thanksgiving. It is a day to gather together as family to give thanks.

Color the picture below. On Thanksgiving Leaves, draw colorful leaves in the bottom right corner and give the sheet to someone with whom you will be eating Thanksgiving dinner.

Thanksgiving • 111

© 2021 Rose Publishing, LLC. Permission to photocopy granted to original purchaser only. *The Super-Sized Book of Holidays, Special Days, & Celebrations.*

Thanksgiving Leaves

To: _____

From: _____

God has given me many things for which to be thankful. You are one of them.

Happy Thanksgiving!

Festival of Lights

You light a lamp for me. The LORD, my God, lights up my darkness. **Psalm 18:28**

What It's All About

In ancient times, a tyrant named Antiochus wanted the Jews to give up their holy books and to worship idols instead of God. The Jewish Maccabees fought Antiochus and won. *Hanukkah* is an eight-day Jewish Festival that celebrates the cleansing of the Temple after its desecration by Antiochus. It is also called the Festival of Lights or the Feast of Dedication.

The Jews rejoiced and returned to their Temple to re-kindle the eternal light in the Temple lamp. This special lamp (or candlestick) was called the *menorah*. It was made of pure gold and had seven branches to hold seven flames. When the Maccabees returned to the Temple, they could only find a very small jar of holy oil for the lamp.

This small amount of oil was only enough to burn for one night. They put the oil in the lamp and a strange thing happened. It burned for eight days! Today, Jewish people celebrate by lighting one candle on the menorah each night, singing special songs, eating foods fried in oil, giving gifts, and playing with dreidels (spinning tops).

Find the eight Stars of David (six-pointed star) and color them blue. Then, color the picture.

Dreidel Game

Your word is a lamp to guide my feet and a light for my path. **Psalm 119:105**

What It's All About

Hanukkah celebrates the Jewish victory against the tyrant Antiochus. After their win, they went to light the holy Temple lamp called the *menorah*. They only had enough oil for one night, but the lamp stayed lit for eight days!

Today, Jewish families celebrate this festival by lighting the candles on their *menorah* and by having parties with gifts, singing, celebrating, and lots of potato pancakes for everyone to eat. It's very possible that even Jesus celebrated Hanukkah (see John 10:22).

Children are given little spinning tops called dreidels as part of the celebration. Each side of the dreidel has a Hebrew letter of NGHS, which represent the saying "*Nes gadol haya sham,*" or "A great miracle happened there." In Israel, a letter is replaced so the phrase says "A great miracle happened here."

What You Need for Younger Children

- Dreidel Board (p. 115) • Dreidel • Paper • Crayons or markers

Preparation

Photocopy Dreidel Board, making one copy for every five players.

What Younger Children Do

1. Divide into groups of five players.
2. Determine how many rounds or how long you are going to play.
3. On your turn, spin the dreidel in the center of the Dreidel Board.
4. When it stops spinning, write down the number to which the top of dreidel points.
5. After a certain number of turns, or length of time, add up the numbers.
6. Whoever has the greatest number of points recites, or chooses someone to recite, the memory verse.

What You Need for Older Children

- Dreidel • Game pieces (chocolate coins, chocolate chips, raisins, pennies, etc.)

What Older Children Do

1. Divide into groups of any number and sit in a circle.
2. Each player begins with ten game pieces. The goal is to get the most game pieces by spinning the dreidel.
3. At the beginning of each round, players put one game piece in the center. Every time the center is empty, each player contributes a game piece.
4. On your turn, spin the dreidel once.
   - If *Nun* is facing up, take nothing.
   - If *Gimel* is facing up, take everything in the center.
   - If *Hey* is facing up, take half. If there is an uneven number in the middle, take half plus one game piece.
   - If *Shin* is facing up, add a game piece to the center. (In Israel, this letter would be *Peh*).
5. If a player runs out of game pieces, they are either out of the game or they may ask another player for a loan.
6. The first person to collect all the game pieces, or when time is up, may recite, or ask someone else to recite, the memory verse.

Bonus: Make Your Own Dreidel

Search online to find tutorials for making your own dreidels.

Dreidel Board

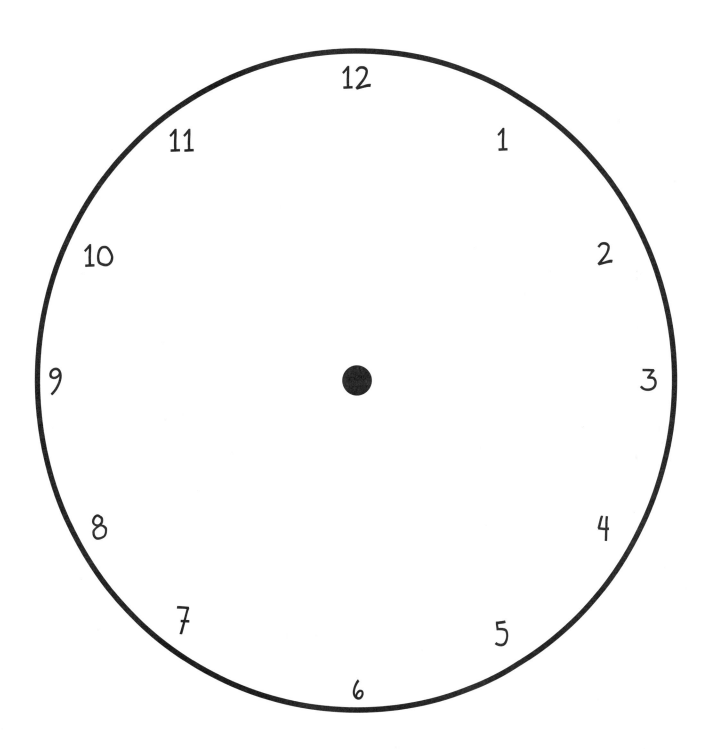

Advent Giving Tree

Remember the words of the Lord Jesus: "It is more blessed to give than to receive." **Acts 20:35**

What You Need
- Advent Tree (p. 117) • Red and green construction paper • Scissors • Crayons or markers
- Decorative elements (glitter, pom-poms, wiggle eyes, stickers, etc.) • Tape

Preparation
Photocopy this page on red paper, making one for each child. Photocopy the Advent Tree on green construction paper, making one for each child.

What It's All About
The ornaments on the Advent tree are numbered, and each one has something you should do on that day, starting with December first.

What to Do
Help children share the spirit of Christmas with an Advent Giving Tree.

1. Cut out twenty-four circles. These are the ornaments.
2. Decorate the ornaments with various colors and designs.
3. Tape the top of each circle to the tree so that when the circle is lifted, it reveals what is written underneath.
4. Put your Advent Tree somewhere you'll see it everyday. Each day of December, lift up your ornament to see how you can spread God's love this season.

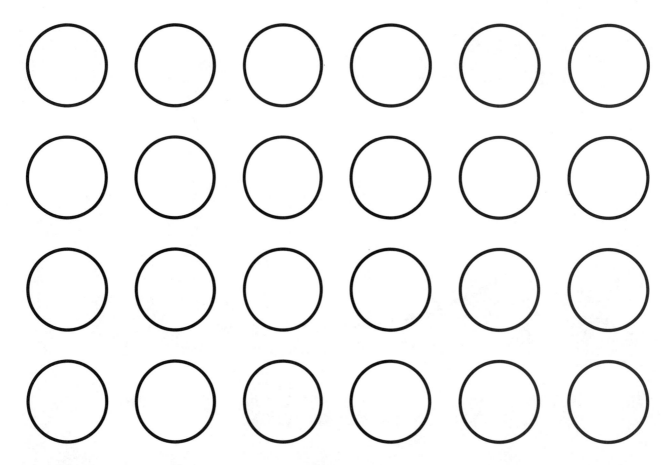

116 • Advent

Advent Tree

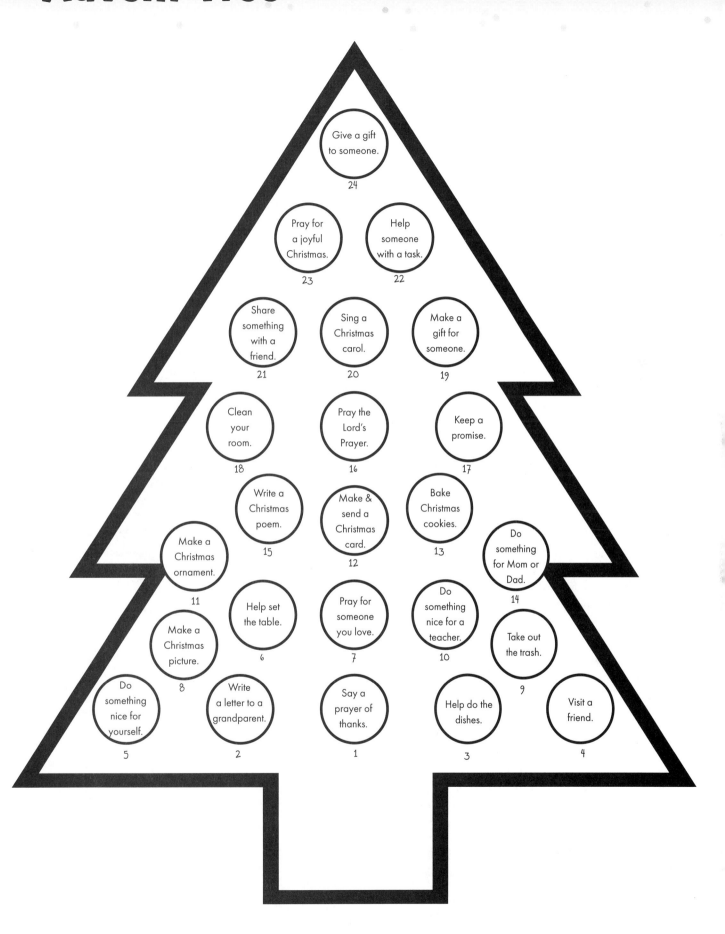

Family Advent Wreath

All honor and glory to God forever and ever! He is the eternal King, the unseen one who never dies; he alone is God. Amen. **1 Timothy 1:17**

What You Need for Each Family

- Marker • Heavy cardboard circle cake board, at least 12-to 14-inches in diameter • Scissors
- Thin wire • Ruler • Several green boughs (cedar, pine, etc.) • Kitchen shears • 4 red or purple candles
- 1 white candle • Glue • Christmas decor (red beads, small ornaments, ribbons, etc.) • Tacky glue or self-hardening clay

Preparation

Photocopy this page, making one for each family. Plan an evening in late November, before the beginning of Advent, when families can come together for a time of fellowship.

What It's All About

What a wonderful time of year to develop the important habit of having family devotions. During this evening, each family will work together to make their own Advent wreath to use at home during the coming weeks until Christmas.

What to Do

1. Write your family name and the year on the back of your cardboard base.
2. Make small holes in the cardboard in order to slip thin wire through to tie on the boughs. Do not cut out the center of the cardboard; you will need this to hold candles.
3. Draw five circles in the center of the cardboard to mark where you'll glue the candles. Trace the base of one candle in the center of the cardboard and space the other four holes about two to three inches away.
4. Using the kitchen shears, trim the boughs as desired. Shape boughs into a circle and wire them to the cardboard base.
5. Use tacky glue or self-hardening clay to keep the white candle in the center circle. Place the other candles in the remaining circles.
6. Decorate the wreath with assorted Christmas decor of your choice.
7. Cut along the dashed line below and keep the Family Advent Wreath Devotion near your wreath. Follow the guide each week to celebrate Advent with your family.

Family Advent Wreath Devotion

The Advent wreath is a wonderful Christmas symbol. The circle, with no beginning and no end, stands for the eternity of God. The evergreens represent life and growth. The five candles represent the four Sundays of Advent and the day of Jesus' birth. Red represents the blood Jesus shed for us. White represents the purity of Jesus.

Week 1: Light the first candle: Prophecy Candle. Read Isaiah 7:14 and Isaiah 9:2–6. Sing "O Come, O Come, Emmanuel" and "It Came Upon the Midnight Clear."

Week 2: Light the first and second candles: Bethlehem Candle. Read Micah 5:2–4. Sing "O Little Town of Bethlehem" and "The First Noel."

Week 3: Light first, second, and third candles: Shepherd's Candle. Read Luke 2:8–20. Sing "Go Tell It on the Mountain."

Week 4: Light first, second, third, and fourth candles: Star and Angel Candle. Read Matthew 2:1–12. Sing "Hark! The Herald Angels Sing."

Christmas Eve: Light the first four plus the center white candle: Christ Candle. Read Luke 2:1–20. Sing "Joy to The World" and "O Come, All Ye Faithful."

Angels Appear

When I am afraid, I will put my trust in [God]. **Psalm 56:3**

What It's All About

Angels played an important part in the story of Christmas. An angel came to Mary and told her she would have a baby. The angel told her not to be afraid because her son would be great. Mary had pleased God.

An angel appeared to Joseph and told him to take Mary as his wife and to not be afraid. Then the angel told him that the baby would be called Jesus. The angel said Jesus would save his people from their sins.

Many angels appeared to the shepherds on the hillside the night Jesus was born in Bethlehem. They sang, "Glory to God in the highest, and on Earth peace and good will." Angels have appeared at various times throughout the Bible, but none were quite as glorious as the ones that announced Jesus' birth.

Let's complete the dot-to-dot and color this picture to remember this important part of the Christmas story. Write answers to the questions on the lines provided.

Discussion Questions

1. What did the angel tell Mary?

   _____

   _____

2. What did the angel tell Joseph?

   _____

   _____

3. Why did the angels appear to the shepherds?

   _____

   _____

The Candy Cane Story

The Lord is God! He made us, and we are his. We are his people, the sheep of his pasture. **Psalm 100:3**

What It's All About

The candy cane is one of the most popular candies at Christmastime. Did you know that this sugary treat is actually a symbol of Jesus? In the late seventeenth century, a German choirmaster gave out white sugar sticks to fidgety choir boys. This was supposed to keep them quiet during the long and solemn church services.

But some of the church members did not think it was appropriate to have candy in church. So the choirmaster bent the candy into a shepherd's staff. The candy cane wasn't just candy anymore. It was a religious symbol, which made the church members happy.

As the years passed, the candy cane became more popular and began to have more symbols. The pure white color symbolizes the virgin birth and the sinless nature of Jesus. The hardness of the candy symbolizes the solid rock of Jesus Christ on which the church was founded and the unwavering promises of God.

The shape of the cane represents the staff of our Good Shepherd, Jesus. The cane also represents the staff of the shepherds who were the first to worship the newborn Christ. But most importantly, the cane when turned upside down is the letter representing the precious name of Jesus.

In the twentieth century, red stripes and a peppermint flavor were added. The red became a symbol for Jesus' blood that he shed on the cross. The flavor and aroma of peppermint is likened to hyssop, a sweet-smelling herb. In Bible times, hyssop was used for its savory taste and as a medicine.

Any time you see a candy cane, allow it to remind you what Christmas is all about: Jesus, the only reason for the season. Color the picture and answer the questions on the blank lines provided.

Discussion Questions

1. Why did the choirmaster change the shape of the sugar candy?

   _____

   _____

2. What do the red and white colors represent?

   _____

   _____

3. How is Jesus like a shepherd?

   _____

   _____

Sweet Candy Canes Bouquet

The LORD is my shepherd; I have all that I need. **Psalm 23:1**

What You Need

- Candy Cane Patterns (p. 122) • White card stock • Scissors • Red and white pipe cleaners
- White or red and white striped drinking straws • Ruler • Red and white tissue paper
- Glue • Hole punch • Yarn • Crayons or markers

Preparation

Photocopy Candy Cane Patterns onto card stock, making one for every two children. Cut page in half to separate candy canes.

What It's All About

Do you like candy? Most everyone likes some kind of candy. But why? Usually it is because of the sweet taste.

At Christmastime, there are many kinds of candy to enjoy as we celebrate. A traditional favorite is the candy cane. We hang candy canes on our trees and decorate our homes with them, as well as just eat them.

The candy cane's shape is a reminder of the staff the shepherds may have carried the night they left their flocks and went to find baby Jesus. The red and white colors on the candy cane remind us that Jesus was born to be our Savior. His red blood washes our sins white as snow. The sweet flavor of the candy cane can remind us of Jesus' gentle, pleasing spirit.

What To Do

Make a bouquet of candy canes by following the instructions below. At the end, tie the Pipe Cleaner Candy Canes and the Curvy Straw Candy Canes together with yarn to make a bouquet. Attach the Tissue Candy Cane as the note.

Pipe Cleaner Candy Canes

1. Twist one red and one white pipe cleaner around each other.
2. Bend the top down to look like a candy cane.

Curvy Straw Candy Canes

1. Cut a drinking straw into several ½-inch pieces.
2. Slide the pieces over two red pipe cleaners leaving a ½-inch space between each straw.
3. Bend the top portion into a cane shape.

Tissue Candy Canes

1. Write the memory verse on the back of the candy cane.
2. Mark off sections of the candy cane with diagonal slashes about 1 inch apart.
3. Cut several 1x1-inch squares of red tissue paper.
4. Fill every other section of the cane with glue.
5. Crumple and set the red tissue squares in the glue until they fill in the whole section.
6. Repeat steps 3–5 using white tissue paper.
7. Punch a hole on the top of the candy cane and tie a loop of red yarn through it.

Candy Cane Patterns

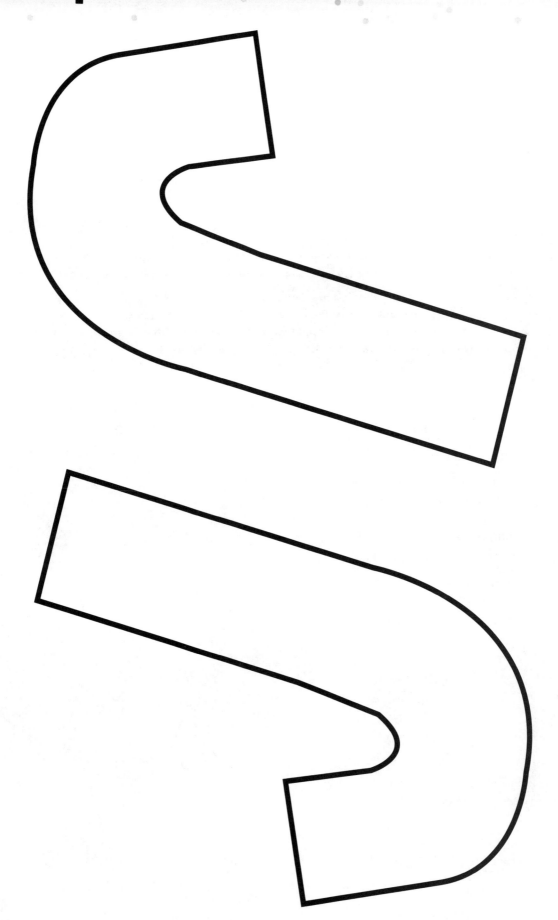

122 • Christmas

Circle of Love

Long ago the LORD said to Israel: "I have loved you, my people, with an everlasting love. With unfailing love I have drawn you to myself. **Jeremiah 31:3**

What It's All About

A festive evergreen wreath is a symbol of Christmas. In the United States, many are made with balsam and cedar boughs. The boughs are bundled and hauled to factories where wreath makers break them into small, fragrant bunches, and wire them to a metal ring. When the circle is full, pine cones, decorations, and bows are added. The wreaths are then ready to be shipped all over the United States for people to buy.

The use of evergreen to make a wreath reminds us that God's love is everlasting. The wreath is shaped like a circle to signify that God has always loved us and he will continue to love us. When you see a wreath this Christmas season, think of God's everlasting love.

What To Do

Choose which type of wreath to make. Then have children follow the numbered steps.

What You Need for a Large Tissue and Wire Wreath

• Wire hanger, one for each child • Scissors • Green tissue paper • Red ribbon • Glue

1. Pull the wire hanger into a circle shape with the hook at the top.
2. Cut several strips of green tissue paper into 2x8-inch strips. Measurements don't need to be exact.
3. Fold a piece of tissue in half over the wire, give it one twist, and slide it to the top where the hook is. Repeat the method around the entire circle, pushing the tissues tightly together.
4. Cut a 6-inch piece of ribbon.
5. Tie the ribbon in a bow and glue it to the top center of the wreath.

Optional: Add red sequins or pom-poms for berries on the wreath.

What You Need for a Small Lace and Ribbon Wreath

• Scissors • Ruler • Green lace • Wire cutter • Craft wire, 18- or 20-gauge • Red ribbon • Glue • Ornament hook

Preparation

Use scissors to cut a 12-inch length of green lace. Use wire cutter to cut an 8-inch length of craft wire, making one for each child.

What To Do

1. Thread the wire through the top hem of the lace.
2. Pull the lace into a circle and tie the wire in a knot. Clip the ends.
3. Tie a 6-inch piece of red ribbon into a bow and glue it to the top.
4. Add an ornament hook at the top for hanging.

Candle Wreath

Let your good deeds shine out for all to see, so that everyone will praise your heavenly Father. **Matthew 5:16**

What You Need

- Candle Wreath Patterns (p. 125) • Card stock • Scissors • Paper plate • Yellow or orange crayons or markers
- Glue • Green tissue paper • Red pom-poms • Hole punch • White and red ribbon or yarn

Preparation

Photocopy Candle Wreath Patterns onto card stock, making one for each child. Make a finished project for children to use as an example.

What It's All About

Read the Meaning of the Wreath to the children.

At Christmas we see many doors with wreaths. Did you know that every part of the wreath represents something about God? We are going to make our own wreaths as a reminder that Jesus is the reason for the season!

What To Do

1. Fold a paper plate in half and cut out the center of the paper plate.
2. Cut out the candle and color the flame of the candle yellow or orange.
3. Glue the base of the candle to the paper plate so that the flame is approximately in the center of the wreath hole.
4. Cut tissue paper into approximately 3-inch squares.
5. Crunch the tissue paper squares and glue then onto the paper plate wreath. Continue until the whole plate is covered.
6. Glue red pom-pom onto the wreath to represent berries.
7. Make a white bow out of ribbon or yarn and glue it to the bottom of the wreath.
8. Cut out the Meaning of the Wreath explanation and hole punch where indicated.
9. Thread a piece of red yarn through the hole and tie the explanation to the wreath.

Candle Wreath Patterns

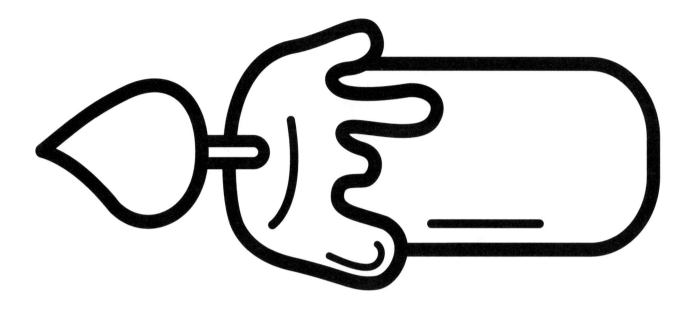

Meaning of the Wreath

A wreath is round and reminds us of God. God is eternal (1 Timothy 1:17), with no beginning nor end.

The candle reminds us that Christ is the light of the world (John 3:19), so we, too, are to let our lights shine (Matthew 5:16).

Green represents life and hope, and Jesus is the hope of the world (Joel 3:16).

Red berries remind us that the Lord Jesus died on the cross and shed his blood so that our sins would be forgiven.

The white bow reminds us that Jesus has forgiven (or cleansed) us of our sins so that we may have life eternal.

Pop Up Nativity

The Lord himself will give you the sign. Look! The virgin will conceive a child! She will give birth to a son and will call him Immanuel (which means "God is with us"). **Isaiah 7:14**

What You Need

- Nativity Patterns (p. 127) • Crayons or markers • Scissors • Glue • Craft stick, one for each child • Modeling clay

Preparation

Photocopy Nativity Patterns onto card stock, making one for each child.

What It's All About

For hundreds of years, God's people waited for their Messiah. Prophets (special messengers from God) told about things that would happen when the Messiah came. One of those signs was that a virgin would have a baby.

Mary was a virgin when the angel Gabriel told her that God chose her to be the mother of the Messiah. This was a big deal! God chose her because she was faithful to him. Even when she and her husband, Joseph, had to travel to Bethlehem, she had faith that God would take care of them.

Bethlehem was overcrowded with travelers. Joseph could not find a room for them anywhere. But then, an inn keeper offered them the room where he kept his animals. When Jesus was born, Mary did not have a crib for him, so she put him on the hay of a feeding trough. This is called a *manger*.

Shepherds came to see baby Jesus and were amazed at what they saw. Some time later, wise men from the East followed a star to see Jesus. They offered him gifts and worshiped him.

Today, we can make our own nativity scene as a reminder of Jesus' birth.

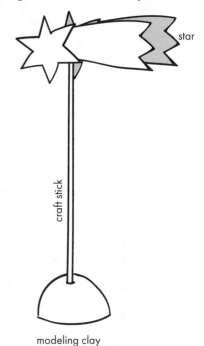

What To Do

1. Color the Nativity Patterns.
2. Cut out the Nativity Patterns.
3. Apply glue to one side of Mary and Joseph's tunics. Then connect the opposite side, so that both figures stand up on their own.
4. Cut a small slit over Mary's arms where indicated.
5. Slip Jesus's tab through the slit in Mary's arms.
6. Glue the stars to the top of a craft stick.
7. Make a small ball of modeling clay.
8. Once the glue has dried, place the craft stick into the modeling clay as illustrated.
9. Fold the manger along the indicated lines so that it stands up on its own. You can decide to keep Jesus in Mary's arms or put him in the manger.
10. Set up your nativity scene.

Nativity Patterns

- - - - - cut
· · · · · fold

Christmas • 127

Christmas Gift Pockets

If you sinful people know how to give good gifts to your children, how much more will your heavenly Father give good gifts to those who ask him. **Matthew 7:11**

What You Need

• Scissors • Yarn • Measuring tape • Tape • Christmas card fronts, two for each child • Hole punch

Preparation

Cut a strand of yarn approximately 40–48 inches long, making one for each child. Wrap tape around one end of each yarn length to make a needle.

What It's All About

Christmas is a time for giving and receiving gifts. We spend lots of time looking for just the right gift to give someone we love. Or maybe we take the time to make a special gift. It is so much fun to see the look on someone's face as they unwrap the pretty paper to reveal the treasure that we have chosen!

Parents love to give gifts to their children. Because they love their children, they want to give them the best they can afford.

In Matthew 7, Jesus tells us that God, our heavenly Father, wants to give good gifts to his children. We are his children, and he wants the best for us. The greatest gift that was ever given was a gift from God. It was the gift of his Son, Jesus, who was sent to Earth and born in a manger.

What To Do

1. Select two large Christmas card fronts.
2. Trim the cards to the same size by holding them together and rounding the corners with scissors.
3. Hold the blank sides together and punch holes along both sides and along the bottom. Don't hole punch the top.
4. Take a pre-cut length of yarn and weave it through the top-most hole on the left side of the card. Continue weaving the yarn through the holes around the cards sides and bottom. Leave a 6-inch tail.
5. Tie the extra yarn at the top to make a handle.

Optional: Stuff a small gift or candy inside the pocket and give it to someone special.

Christmas Winter Fun

Purify me from my sins, and I will be clean; wash me, and I will be whiter than snow. **Psalm 51:7**

What It's All About

Did you know that half the world celebrates Christmas in the winter? Winter snow reminds us that Jesus came to save us from our sins and wash us white as snow. In the snow globe below, draw Jesus in a manger. Then, complete the fun winter activities around the snow globe. Remember that Jesus is the true reason to celebrate this season.

Christmas Tree Puzzle

The Savior—yes, the Messiah, the Lord—has been born today in Bethlehem, the city of David! **Luke 2:11**

What You Need
- Bibles • Crayons or markers

Preparation
Photocopy this page, making one for each child.

What It's All About
A Christmas tree is one of the most famous symbols of Christmas. It's usually decorated in lights to remind us that Jesus is the light of the world. The Christmas Tree Puzzle is full of Christmas things, too. Use the clues to fill out the tree.

What To Do
Read the numbered clues below and write your answers in the tree boxes. Put one letter in each box. If the clue stumps you, look up the Bible reference.

1. God loved the world: He gave his one and only Son, _____ that everyone who believes in him will not perish, but have eternal life. **John 3:16**
2. The Son's father was _____. **John 3:16**
3. His mother was _____. **Luke 2:5,7**
4. His name was _____. **Matthew 1:21**
5. His bed was a _____. **Luke 2:7**
6. The angels sang _____. **Luke 2:13**
7. _____, the angel was joined by a vast host of other angels. **Luke 2:13**
8. The first ones to hear of his birth were _____. **Luke 2:8–11**
9. The town where he was born was _____. **Luke 2:4,11**

CHRISTMAS

Special Visitor Code

For God has not given us a spirit of fear and timidity, but of power, love, and self-discipline. **2 Timothy 1:7**

What You Need
- Crayons or markers

Preparation
Photocopy this page, making one for each child.

What To Do
To fill in the blanks, find the letter in the circle or circles with the same number that is under the blank. Example: 3,4 = J. Color the angel.

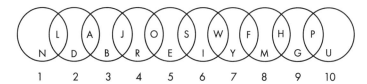

One day ____ ____ ____ sent the ____ ____ ____ ____ ____
         9   4,5   2   2,3   1   9   5   1,2

____ ____ ____ ____ ____ ____ ____ to ____ ____ ____ ____. "Do not be
 9   2,3   3   4   6   5   1,2   8   2,3   4   7

____ ____ ____ ____ ____ ____," he said. "God will give you a ____ ____ ____ ____
 2,3   7,8   4   2,3   6   2   3   2,3   3   7

____ ____ ____. He will be the ____ ____ ____ of the Most ____ ____ ____ ____."
 3   4,5   7   5,6   4,5   1   8,9   6   9   8,9

Mary said, ____ ____ ____ it be as you have ____ ____ ____ ____."
            8   2,3   7   5,6   2,3   6   2

Mary was pledged to marry ____ ____ ____ ____ ____ ____. An angel came to him in a
                          3,4   4,5   5,6   5   9,10 8,9

____ ____ ____ ____ ____, saying, "Do not be afraid to take Mary as your
 2   4   5   2,3   8

____ ____ ____ ____ God gave her the ____ ____ ____ ____ Call his name
 6,7   6   7,8   5   3   2,3   3   7

____ ____ ____ ____ ____. He will save people from their ____ ____ ____ ____."
 3,4   5   5,6   10   5,6   5,6   6   1   5,6

Christmas Poem

I will praise the LORD as long as I live. **Psalm 146:2**

What You Need
- Crayons or markers

Preparation
Photocopy this page, making one for each child.

What To Do
Choose words from the box to supply the missing words in this rhyme about Jesus' birth.

angel	boy	Earth	head	lay	'round	swaddling
bed	child	found	inn	mother	say	tidings
birth	do	hay	joy	rejoicing	star	too

Christmas, Christmas, Christmas! Here's what the letters _____:

C is for the Christ _____ who in the manger _____.

H is for the cattle's _____ that pillowed Jesus' _____.

R is for _____ by those around his _____.

I is for a busy _____, where room could not be _____.

S is for the _____ cloths that wrapped the baby _____.

T is for good _____ that brought such wondrous _____.

M is for the _____ dear who watched her baby _____.

A is for the _____ host who told of peace on _____.

S is for the _____ so bright that shone at Jesus' _____.

Wishing you a merry Christmas and a happy New Year, _____.

May you honor Jesus in everything you _____.

Wise Men Maze

When the Spirit of truth comes, he will guide you into all truth. **John 16:13**

What You Need
- Crayons or markers

Preparation
Photocopy this page, making one for each child.

What It's All About
The wise men from the East traveled far to find Jesus. They followed a star to Judea, but they weren't sure exactly where to find Jesus. Who did they think would know where the Messiah was born? They asked King Herod. King Herod was not happy to hear that a new king had been born. He was afraid that Jesus would try to steal his throne. King Herod told the wise men they would find the new king in Bethlehem. The wise men were so thankful! But King Herod asked them to return to him once they had found Jesus. He lied and said that he also wanted to worship the new king, but really he wanted to kill him. God warned the wise men in a dream not to return to King Herod.

What To Do
Help the wise men travel to King Herod, and then to Jesus. Finally, help the wise men get home by another route. Remember, they don't want to see King Herod again!

Shepherds Search for Jesus

I love all who love me. Those who search will surely find me. **Proverbs 8:17**

What You Need
- Crayons or markers

Preparation
Photocopy this page, making one for each child.

What It's All About
One NIGHT there were SHEPHERDS in the FIELDS, keeping WATCH over their FLOCKS. An ANGEL of the LORD appeared to them, and the GLORY of the Lord shone around them. They were terrified. But the angel said, "Don't be AFRAID. I bring you GOOD NEWS of great JOY that will be for all PEOPLE. Today in the TOWN of BETHLEHEM a SAVIOR has been BORN; He IS CHRIST the Lord. You will FIND a baby wrapped in swaddling clothes lying in a MANGER." Suddenly a great HEAVENLY HOST appeared with the angel, praising God and saying, "Glory to God in the highest."

When the angels left, the shepherds said, "Let's GO and SEE this thing that has happened. So they hurried off and found MARY and JOSEPH. The BABY was lying in the manger.

What To Do

For younger elementary children: In the word search, find only the capitalized words not underlined from the story.

For older elementary children: In the word search, find all the capitalized and underlined words. Note: the underlined words are hidden diagonally.

```
H B K F S O M E Y X G O O D F
C E D I B A S A A F R A I D I
J T S N A A V W R F Q W Z M E
O H P D B G W I B Y X R R M L
Y L G O Y V J J O I B O R N D
J E L S H E P H E R D S H G S
O H O S C D O D B H T X N L I
S E R E C C A E S E G X I C U
E M Y E N S L K D A P Z G H M
P N C S F P C O H V S W H R S
H F W Y O O R K G E T J T I S
D E F E L K O Z O N U O E S R
N N P F A N G E L L I T W T H
X B L O R D T X F Y C A X N M
W A T C H H O S T M A N G E R
```

Why Jesus Came Maze

*Give thanks to the L*ORD*, for he is good! His faithful love endures forever.* **1 Chronicles 16:34**

What You Need
- Crayons or markers

Preparation
Photocopy this page, making one for each child.

What It's All About
Jesus loves you very much, and he came to Earth for one very special reason. Complete the maze to find that reason.

What To Do
Find a path through the maze from Heaven to Earth and write the letters in the blanks.

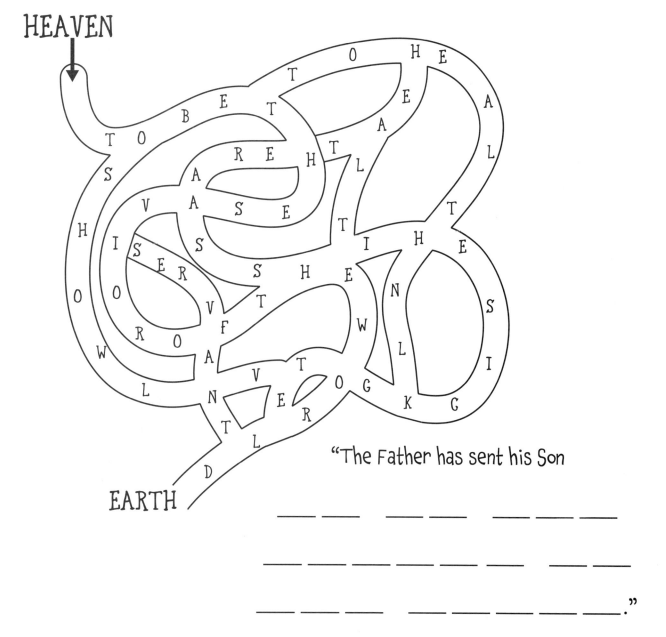

"The Father has sent his Son

___ ___ ___ ___ ___ ___ ___

___ ___ ___ ___ ___ ___

___ ___ ___ ___ ___ ___ ."

1 John 4:14

Christmas Plan-Ahead Program

For the LORD is good. His unfailing love continues forever, and his faithfulness continues to each generation. **Psalm 100:5**

What You Need

- Bible character costumes (bathrobes, towels, fluffy coats [for sheep], etc.) • Camera

Preparation

Christmas programs are often hectic to produce when December arrives, and the participants never get to see the program. In order to help lessen the rush of the season, prepare for the Christmas program ahead of time by taking pictures.

Early in the fall, make arrangements with a local farm for a photo shoot. If this is not possible, create a suitable backdrop. Get creative! Ask the children to draw the backgrounds, or ask church volunteers to help create one.

What to Do

1. Children pose in costumes depicting various scenes from the Christmas story: angels appearing to Mary and Joseph; Joseph leading a donkey carrying Mary or the two of them walking down a dirt road; angels appearing to shepherds with their sheep; angels and shepherds kneeling in the straw around Mary and baby Jesus. Be sure that all the children get to be in one of the pictures.
2. Take pictures of each scene from different angles so that you will have several to choose from to best present the story.
3. When the pictures are printed, children help determine which ones to use for the program.
4. Children record the Christmas story narrative and several Christmas hymns to accompany the story.
5. Create your program presentation by combining the pictures and songs.
6. When the day arrives for the program presentation, children can sit with their families and friends and see themselves portraying the nativity story.

Alternate Idea: Nativity Book

When multiple copies of the pictures are printed, children create their own nativity book. Fold a few sheets of paper in half and staple them along the fold. Glue pictures onto the pages and write one sentence descriptions of the scenes. Share the book with family or friends.

Christmas Celebration

Glory to God in highest heaven, and peace on earth to those with whom God is pleased. **Luke 2:14**

What It's All About
Christmas is a festive time of year that can sometimes be taken over by Santa, Rudolph, and Frosty. Let's focus on the real reason for this holiday—celebrating the long-awaited Savior's birth!

What to Do
A Sunday school party will provide a meaningful time of celebration and sharing of the Christmas message. Instead of bringing gifts to exchange with each other, ask each child to bring a gift that can be given to a child in a needy family or children's home. Play games, have refreshments, and include a Bible lesson during your party. The children could go Christmas caroling around the church and then return to the classroom for refreshments. Following are some suggested activities.

Christmas Story Scramble
- Paper • Scissors • Box

Search online for Luke 2:1–12. Copy and paste the text into a document, omitting the verse numbers, and double space it. Cut the story line by line into as many pieces as there are children. Scramble the verses in a box.

Children draw one phrase out of the box. The object of the game is to put the verses into the correct order. Children arrange themselves in order according to the verse or phrase they have. When everyone is in line, children read the story in the proper order.

Balloon Pop
- Crayons or markers • Paper • Scissors • Balloons

Make a list of basic questions about the Christmas story with a few fun questions mixed in. Write each question on a slip of paper and insert it into a balloon. Blow up the balloons and tie them around the room. Children take turns finding a balloon, popping it, and answering the question. This will not only liven up the party, but will help you to know where the children are in their knowledge of the Christmas story. The other children will be the judges as to the correctness of the answers.

Christmas Dinner Game
In planning this feast remember that the cook is fussy and does not like *P*s. Players take turns naming something to have for dinner. Anyone who names a food containing the letter *P* is out. After a certain set of time, the remaining players recite the memory verse together.

Make a Nativity Booklet
- 12x18-inch construction paper
- Crayons or markers • Stapler

Photocopy the nativity coloring pages on pages 142–146, and 10–11. Children make a cover by folding a sheet of construction paper in half. Children decorate the cover, put the coloring pages in order, and then place the pages inside the cover. Children staple the book along the edge to secure. Children color pages as time allows. Encourage them to share the pages and the story with their families.

Prophecies of the Messiah

All of us, like sheep, have strayed away. We have left God's paths to follow our own. Yet the Lord laid on him the sins of us all. **Isaiah 53:6**

What You Need

- Bibles • Crayons or markers

What It's All About

God revealed his plan for the Messiah through his prophets. Prophets told God's messages to the Hebrew people. These messages were called prophecies. Many told of things that would happen to the Messiah. Because of these prophecies, the Hebrews were waiting for the Messiah.

Look up the verses below to see which prophecies are pictured on the Christmas tree. Draw a line from the verse to the picture. Then, color the picture.

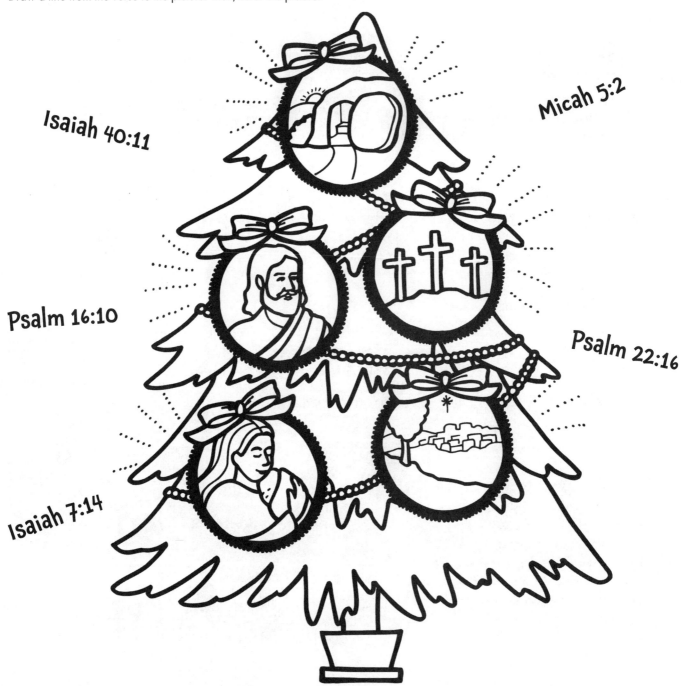

Isaiah 40:11

Micah 5:2

Psalm 16:10

Psalm 22:16

Isaiah 7:14

The Symbol of the Candy Cane

Even when I walk through the darkest valley, I will not be afraid, for you are close beside me. Your rod and your staff protect and comfort me. **Psalm 23:4**

What It's All About

Do you know the meaning of the candy cane? The candy cane helps remind us what Christmas is all about—the life, death, and resurrection of God's Son, Jesus. The red and white colors remind us of Jesus' blood which washes our sins white as snow. The shape looks like a shepherd's staff and reminds us that Jesus is our shepherd. He protects us from harm. The next time you see a candy cane, remember Jesus' birthday.

Color the picture.

Christmas • 139

Christmas Traditions

The light shines in the darkness, and the darkness can never extinguish it. **John 1:5**

What It's All About

Where do all of our Christmas traditions come from? Our traditions began with Jesus' birth over 2,000 years ago. Jesus came into a dark and sinful world that needed a Savior. As the gospel spread around the world, many celebrations and festivities were replaced with Christian holidays. Christmas replaced the Roman December festival called *Saturnalia*. There's no better time than the darkest season of the year to celebrate the light of Jesus!

Color the picture.

Christmas Symbols

God promised this Good News long ago through his prophets in the holy Scriptures. **Romans 1:2**

What It's All About

At Christmastime it's fun to write letters to Santa, decorate with ornaments, and eat tasty desserts and candy canes. The shape of the candy cane reminds us of a shepherd's staff. Jesus is our Good Shepherd, and as Christians, we should always remember the best Christmas gift; that God sent his only son to Earth. Remember as you get caught up in the excitement and glitter of Christmas that Jesus is the only true reason to celebrate. He is the best news that the world has ever received!

Color the picture.

The Angel Visits Mary

Gabriel appeared to her and said, "Greetings, favored woman! The Lord is with you!" Luke 1:28

What It's All About

God sent the angel Gabriel to tell Mary some very important news: she would be the mother of Jesus, God's own Son. Mary was frightened at first by this unusual visitor. But Mary trusted God and accepted the task of mothering Jesus.

Color the picture.

142 • Christmas

© 2021 Rose Publishing, LLC. Permission to photocopy granted to original purchaser only. *The Super-Sized Book of Holidays, Special Days, & Celebrations.*

The Angel Visits Joseph

When Joseph woke up, he did as the angel of the Lord commanded and took Mary as his wife. **Matthew 1:24**

What It's All About

When Mary told Joseph that she was going to have a baby, she and Joseph were not yet married. In Bible times, it was especially shameful for women to be pregnant and unmarried. Joseph wanted to cancel the wedding. But an angel appeared to Joseph in a dream and told him to take Mary as his wife. The angel said the child was God's Son who would save his people from their sins. Color the picture and draw the angel in Joseph's dream.

Christmas • 143

Journey to Bethlehem

He took with him Mary, to whom he was engaged, who was now expecting a child. **Luke 2:5**

What It's All About

The Roman government made a law that all Jews had to pay taxes in the towns from which their families came. Mary and Joseph's families were from Bethlehem, about 70 miles from Nazareth, where they were living. So Mary and Joseph began their journey to Bethlehem.

Color the picture.

At the Inn

She gave birth to her firstborn son. She wrapped him snugly in strips of cloth and laid him in a manger, because there was no lodging available for them. **Luke 2:7**

What It's All About

Mary and Joseph could not find a place to stay in Bethlehem. They traveled for days by foot and donkey to get there. When they arrived, the town was crowded, and there was no room in any of the inns. How do you think Mary and Joseph must have felt when the innkeeper said, "Sorry. No room"?

Color the picture and draw Mary and Joseph's faces as they arrive at the inn door.

Christmas • 145

Born in Bethlehem

You, O Bethlehem, . . . are only a small village among all the people of Judah. Yet a ruler of Israel, whose origins are in the distant past, will come from you. **Micah 5:2**

What It's All About

Mary and Joseph were outcasts in Bethlehem. There was no one to give them a comfortable room so Mary could give birth to her baby. They had no friends or family to help them. All they had was each other and a room where animals were kept.

Color the picture and draw more animals around Mary and Joseph.

Jesus' Birth Announcement

For a child is born to us, a son is given to us. The government will rest on his shoulders. And he will be called: Wonderful Counselor, Mighty God, Everlasting Father, Prince of Peace. **Isaiah 9:6**

What It's All About

Sometimes parents send announcements to their friends and families telling about the birth of their child. Since the birth of Jesus was a very important event, God used angels to announce his birth to the shepherds. Imagine what kind of birth announcement Mary might have used to tell her friends about her newborn Son, Jesus.

Color the picture, draw a stamp on the envelope, and write the information on the lines by looking up the Scriptures.

Baby's Name: _____
Matthew 1:21

Place of Birth: _____
Luke 2:4

Mother's Name: _____
Matthew 1:18

Earthly Father's Name: _____
Matthew 1:20

Father's Name: _____
Luke 1:35

Christmas • 147

An Angel Visits the Shepherds

They were calling out to each other, "Holy, holy, holy is the LORD of Heaven's Armies! The whole earth is filled with his glory!" **Isaiah 6:3**

What It's All About

It was nighttime on the hillsides of Bethlehem. Some poor shepherds were in the fields watching their sheep when suddenly an angel appeared. The whole sky lit up and the shepherds were terrified! The angel told them not to be afraid because he had good news about the birth of Jesus. Before long, the sky was filled with many angels praising God.

Color the picture.

148 • Christmas

Baby Jesus in the Manger

They hurried to the village and found Mary and Joseph. And there was the baby, lying in the manger. **Luke 2:16**

What It's All About

The shepherds were so excited after hearing the good news that they ran to Bethlehem! It was not difficult for them to find the baby. The angel said that Jesus would be wrapped in cloths and lying in a manger. Since newborn babies were not normally put into an animal's feed box, the shepherds must have searched throughout Bethlehem's barns and stables until they found the baby just as the angel said.

Color the picture and draw some shepherds looking into the stable window.

Christmas • 149

Celebrate Christmas Every Day

To all who believed [Jesus] and accepted him, he gave the right to become children of God. **John 1:12**

What It's All About

Christmas is an exciting time of the year with cookie baking, decorating, and gift giving. Most people seem to be extra kind at Christmas. What seems to change people is sometimes called the "Christmas spirit." But the Christmas spirit is really Jesus. He's the one who changes our hearts for goodness and kindness. Jesus wants us to have the Christmas spirit every day, not just once a year.

Color the picture and draw a symbol of Christmas in the boy's heart.

Jesus' Birthday

This is how Jesus the Messiah was born. His mother, Mary . . . became pregnant through the power of the Holy Spirit. **Matthew 1:18**

What It's All About

Christmas is the day that we celebrate Jesus' birthday. We don't know if Bible families celebrated birthdays like we do today. They certainly did not have candles to put on birthday cakes, but they might have had other ways of celebrating. It must have been a joy for Mary and Joseph as they watched their baby, Jesus, grow up.

Color the picture, draw candles on the cake, and give the sheet to someone who does not know about Jesus' birthday.

Happy Birthday, Jesus! Celebrate Jesus' birthday and the salvation that he offers us!

Christmas • 151

The Real Reason

Praise the Lord, the God of Israel, because he has visited and redeemed his people. **Luke 1:68**

What You Need
- Christmas Blessing (p. 153) • Crayons or markers

Preparation
Photocopy this page and Christmas Blessing, making one of each page for each child.

What It's All About

Some Christmas cards focus on Santa Claus, gifts, and candy. But Jesus is the real reason to celebrate Christmas. If you accept God's gift, you can have joy and hope. It is important that you share the hope of Jesus, especially during this time of year.

Color this page. On the Christmas Blessing page, draw baby Jesus in the manger, color the page, and give it to someone who needs to know about Jesus.

Christmas Blessing

To: _____

From: _____

May your Christmas be blessed with the hope, joy, and peace that only Jesus can give.

The Angel's Announcement

There is salvation in no one else! God has given no other name under heaven by which we must be saved. **Acts 4:12**

What You Need
- Angel's Good News (p. 155) • Crayons or markers

Preparation
Photocopy this page and Angel's Good News, making one of each page for each child.

What To Do
Color this page. On the Angel's Good News page, draw a happy face on the angel and give it to someone who needs to hear the good news of Jesus' birth.

Angels announced the good news of Jesus' birth to shepherds on a hillside of Bethlehem.

But the good news of Jesus is for all people everywhere.

Christmas is a time when can tell others about God's Son, Jesus, who came to give us eternal life.

Angel's Good News

To: _____

From: _____

The angel announced
From heaven above:
A Savior is born —
God's gift of love.

May the angel's good news of long ago be a blessing to you this Christmas and throughout the year.

Christmas Around the World

[Jesus] is the sacrifice that atones for our sins—and not only our sins but the sins of all the world. **1 John 2:2**

What You Need
- Star's Light (p. 157) • Crayons or markers

What to Do
Photocopy this page and Star's Light, making one of each page for each child.

What It's All About
People around the world celebrate Christmas in different ways. Americans think of snow, Santa, and jingle bells around Christmas. But children who live in hot places may have never seen snow! Although there are many Christmas traditions, the real reason for Christmas is the same: to celebrate the birth of our Savior, Jesus.

Color this page. On the Star's Light page, draw a star on top of the tree, color the page, and decorate the tree with ornaments. Then give the sheet to a family member.

Star's Light

To: _____

From: _____

May the star on this tree remind you that Jesus is the star that gives light to our world.

Christmas • 157

© 2021 Rose Publishing, LLC. Permission to photocopy granted to original purchaser only. *The Super-Sized Book of Holidays, Special Days, & Celebrations.*

Pottery Puzzle

Give your bodies to God because of all he has done for you. Let them be a living and holy sacrifice—the kind he will find acceptable. This is truly the way to worship him. **Romans 12:1**

What You Need
- Card stock • Crayons or markers • Scissors • Glue

Preparation
Photocopy this page onto card stock, making one for each child.

What It's All About
The new year is the perfect time to refocus our lives on Jesus. Will you let God shape and mold your life this year, as a potter molds a clay pot? He will make something beautiful out of you.

What to Do
1. Color and cut out the puzzle pieces.
2. Glue the pieces in the correct place on the pot to complete the verse.

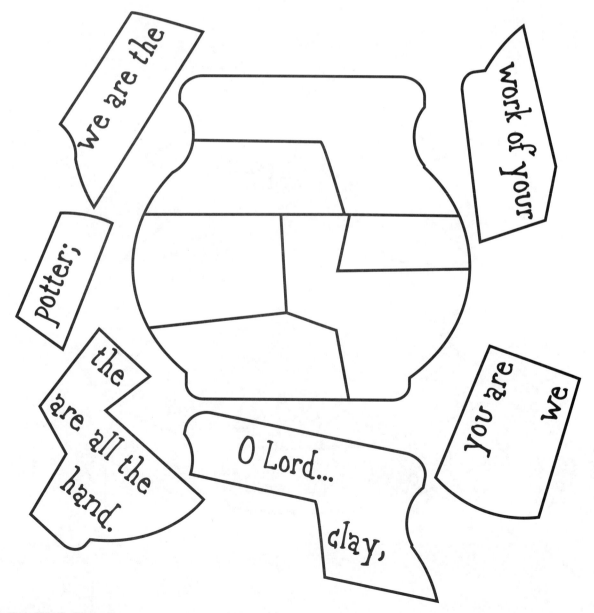

158 • New Year's Day

Spiritual Inventory

Don't copy the behavior and customs of this world, but let God transform you into a new person by changing the way you think. **Romans 12:2**

What You Need
- Crayons or markers

Preparation
Photocopy this page, making one for each child.

What It's All About
It's a brand new year, which means we can make new goals for a better year ahead. Today, you are going to take a spiritual inventory of your own lives as we begin the new year.

What to Do
Answer the following questions about your spiritual life. Color in the thermometer from the bottom up. For each "yes" answer, color up two marks on the thermometer. For every "sometimes" answer, color up one mark. For every "no" answer, don't color. Did you reach the top?

1. Do I pray daily?
2. Do I read my Bible daily?
3. Do I attend Sunday school?
4. Do I give a part of my allowance to God?
5. Do I really love all people everywhere?
6. Do I treat others as I would have them treat me?
7. Do I respect my parents, guardians, and teachers?
8. Am I a good citizen?
9. Do I do my lessons honestly in school?
10. Have I confessed Christ before others? If not, will I receive Christ and witness daily this year?

Based on your thermometer results, what are some spiritual goals that you'd like to make for the new year?

_____

_____

_____

_____

> **Bonus Idea**
> Seal children's spiritual resolutions inside envelopes. Collect the envelopes and keep them until late in the year (or the beginning of the next new year). At that time, return the envelopes so children can see if they achieved the goals they set.

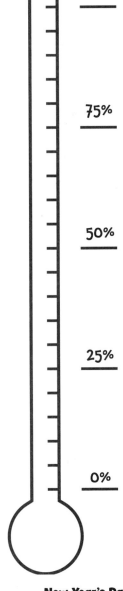

The Promised Land

The land you will soon take over is a land of hills and valleys with plenty of rain—a land that the LORD your God cares for. He watches over it through each season of the year! **Deuteronomy 11:11–12**

What It's All About

When Moses led the Israelites out of Egypt, they wandered in the desert for forty years. Because of their faithlessness, they never saw the new land that God promised them. However, their children did take possession of the land that "flowed with milk and honey." This was a new beginning for the Israelites. God gives us new beginnings, too. Every January we can look forward to what God has in store for us in the coming year.

Color the picture as a reminder of the beautiful land God promised his people and of the new beginnings God gives us.

Happy New Year

This is the day the L<small>ORD</small> has made. We will rejoice and be glad in it. **Psalm 118:24**

What It's All About

New Year's Day is a time to say goodbye to the old year and hello to the new year. It is when we promise ourselves to do better than the year before. God gives us the same opportunity to say goodbye to our sinful ways and hello to the new life we can have in him. Every day can be New Year's Day for Christians because God has given us each new day as a chance to live for him.

Color this picture as a reminder of the new life God gives us. Write your resolutions on the blank lines.

My Dreams Mobile

[Jesus said,] *"I am giving you a new commandment: Love each other. Just as I have loved you, you should love each other."* **John 13:34**

What You Need
• Card stock • Scissors • Crayons or markers • Hole punch • Yarn

Preparation
Photocopy this page on card stock, making four clouds for each child.

What It's All About
Martin Luther King's life mission was for all people to be treated equally. He lead nonviolent protests and marches in the Southern states to get people's attention. In his "I Have a Dream" speech, King spoke of his hope for peaceful communities that did not judge others for their skin color. God does not judge people by how they look. He accepts every one who believes in Jesus.

What To Do
1. Cut out four clouds.
2. Write the memory verse on one cloud.
3. Turn that cloud over to the blank side and write "I Have a Dream" in big letters.
4. On each of the other three clouds, on the lined side, write on separate clouds one dream you have for yourself, one dream for your community, and one dream for the world.
5. Punch a hole at the top of all four clouds where indicated.
6. Punch three holes at the bottom of the "I Have a Dream" cloud.
7. Cut yarn at approximately four-, five-, and six-inch lengths.
8. Tie the yarn to the three dream clouds. Then, tie the other end of the yarn to the verse cloud.
9. Cut and tie a loop of yarn at the top of the verse cloud.
10. Hang your dream mobile where you can see it.

Martin Luther King's Dream

The LORD doesn't see things the way you see them. People judge by outward appearance, but the LORD looks at the heart. **1 Samuel 16:7**

What It's All About

Martin Luther King Jr. was a pastor and civil rights activist. Martin Luther King Jr. gave an inspiring speech called "I Have a Dream." He dreamed that people would not be judged by the color of their skin, but that everyone would be treated equally. God does not judge us by what we look like. He only cares about our heart, or spiritual lives, and how we treat others.

In the dream bubble, write or draw about Martin Luther King's dream.

Martin Luther King Day • 163

Honest Abe Story

We are careful to be honorable before the Lord, but we also want everyone else to see that we are honorable. **2 Corinthians 8:21**

What It's All About

Abraham Lincoln was the sixteenth U.S. president. Lincoln was born in a log cabin in Kentucky. He was a tall, gangly boy who was very intelligent, even though he had little time to go to school because he was helping his family. Lincoln studied and learned everything he could to educate himself.

By the time he was president, Lincoln's best known quality was his honesty. One legend says he walked many miles to return six pennies to a woman he had overcharged as a storekeeper.

Lincoln tried to be fair to everyone. As president, he worked to free enslaved people in America because he believed God created everyone equal. He felt that no one should own another person. Not everyone agreed with him, but Lincoln wanted all people to be treated fairly.

God wants us all to do what is fair and honest. We should always do what's right, even when it's not what's popular.

Color the picture and write answers to the questions on the lines provided.

Discussion Questions

1. Why was Abe Lincoln known for his honesty?

    _____

    _____

2. Why did Lincoln free enslaved people?

    _____

    _____

3. What can we do to please God?

    _____

    _____

Truthful George Story

Don't lie to each other, for you have stripped off your old sinful nature and all its wicked deeds. **Colossians 3:9**

What It's All About

George Washington is known as the father of our country because he was the first U.S. president. Before he became president Washington, he was a surveyor and soldier. Because Washington was the first President of the United States, many people have created myths or stories about him to celebrate his character.

One myth tells a story about Washington as a child. It says that his father once gave him a new hatchet. Washington was a little too eager to try it out and he damaged one of his father's prized cherry trees. Later, when his father called him in and asked who chopped down the tree, George replied, "I cannot tell a lie. . . I did cut it with my hatchet."

Of course, Washington was only human, so he made mistakes like the rest of us. The purpose of this myth is to show the importance of being honest. Still, there are important lessons we can learn from this story.

The Bible tells us that lying is a sin. Even if it seems like lying will help in the short term, lies are wrong and only lead to bigger trouble. If we love God, we don't have to lie. We can always tell God the truth, no matter what.

Color the picture and write answers to the questions on the lines provided.

Discussion Questions

1. Who was George Washington?

   _____

   _____

2. What is lying?

   _____

   _____

3. What should we do instead of lying, even if we're scared of what might happen?

   _____

   _____

Stately Silhouettes

The godly offer good counsel; they teach right from wrong. They have made God's law their own, so they will never slip from his path. **Psalm 37:30–31**

What You Need

- Presidential Profiles (p. 167) • Hall of Fame (p. 168)
- White card stock • Markers • Scissors • Black construction paper
- Poster board • Aluminum foil • Glue • Star stickers

> This craft can be used with either (or both) the Honest Abe and Truthful George stories on pages 164 and 165.

Preparation

On card stock, photocopy Presidential Profiles and Hall of Fame, make a copy of each page for each child.

What It's All About

George Washington was the first president of the United States, and Abe Lincoln was the sixteenth president. Both of them had different challenges during their presidency, but both represent honest leadership. Honesty is important to God. When you make God's law your own, it means that you believe in God's rules and obey them willingly. Let's all strive to be God-following honest leaders.

What To Do

1. Use the patterns to trace and cut one silhouette and one frame from black construction paper.
2. Cover a 7x9-inch piece of poster board with foil paper and glue it in place.
3. Glue the frame over the foil board and glue the silhouette in the center of the oval.
4. Place star stickers on the corners of the frame.
5. Write the memory verse on the back of the frame.

Presidential Profiles

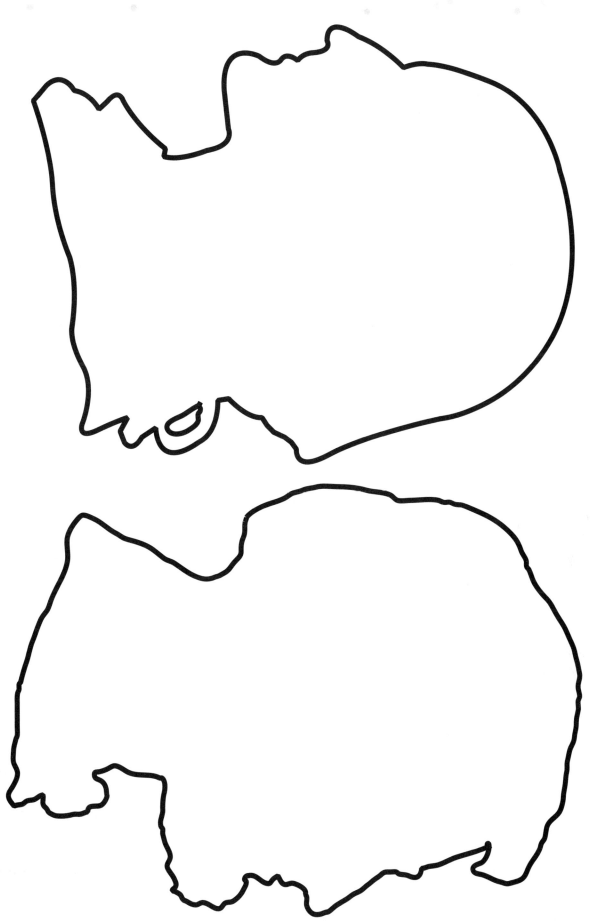

President's Day • 167

Hall of Fame

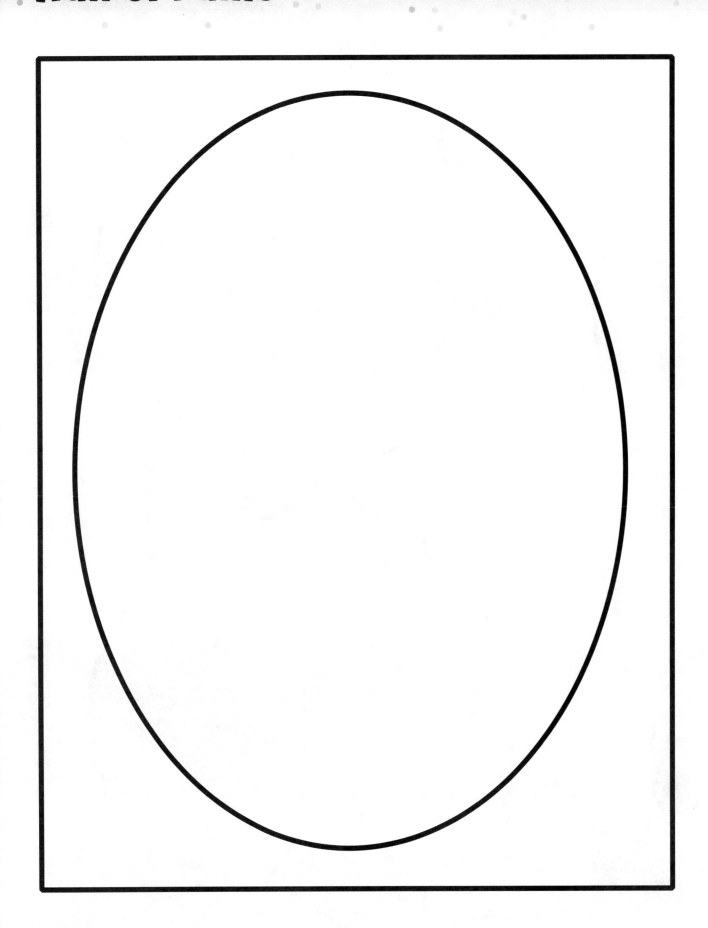

President's Day Celebration

Fix your thoughts on what is true, and honorable, and right, and pure, and lovely, and admirable. Think about things that are excellent and worthy of praise. **Philippians 4:8**

What It's All About

Presidents' Day celebrates the birthdays of two of the greatest presidents in American history: George Washington (the first president) and Abraham Lincoln (the sixteenth president).

What to Do

Plan a patriotic party that emphasizes the value of honesty.

Send an Invitation

Send special red, white, and blue invitations to children in your class a week before the party. Write the following on the invitation:

> *We're having a party. The theme's red, white, and blue.*
> *We want you to come and bring your friends, too.*
> *Time:(whatever time Sunday school starts)*
> *Date:(the Sunday before Presidents' Day)*
> *Place: (wherever your class meets)*

Decorate

Provide a small American flag for each child (be sure to have extras for any visitors who may attend). Decorate the room with red, white, and blue balloons and crepe-paper streamers.

Patriotic Snacks

Serve refreshments such as white frosted cupcakes with red and blue sprinkles on top and red fruit punch.

Money Hunt Game

Cut out rectangles from green construction paper to represent dollar bills. Cut out circles from brown construction paper to represent pennies. Hide an equal number of these pretend coins and dollar bills around the room before the children arrive.

1. Children divide into two groups, the Washingtons and the Lincolns. The Washington group looks for the bills while the Lincoln group looks for the coins. The members of the Washington group must ignore any coins they find, and the Lincoln group must ignore any bills they find.
2. The object is to find as many items as possible in a given length of time.
3. The group that finds the most items recites the memory verse.

Presidents' Stories

Along with your regular lesson for the day, tell a story about one or both of the great presidents whom we are honoring (see pp. 164–165). Close with prayer, asking God to help each child to be a good, honest citizen.

Paper Cone Lilies

Give all your worries and cares to God, for he cares about you. **1 Peter 5:7**

What You Need
- Lily Leaves (p. 171) • Scissors • Ruler • White paper • Tape • Pencils
- Glue • Green construction paper • Crayons or markers

Preparation
Photocopy Lily Leaves, making one for each child, plus one to make an example project for children to follow.

What It's All About

Earth Day is celebrated every year on April 22. It's a special day to clean up and care for God's beautiful world. One of God's beautiful creations is a lily.

A lily is a fragrant white flower that grows on a tall stem. It has pointed green leaves. The petals are soft and fragile. It gives off a wonderful smell. Inside the flower are delicate yellow stamen.

In the gospel of Matthew, Jesus used lilies as an example when he was teaching. He said, "I tell you not to worry about everyday life—whether you have enough food and drink, or enough clothes to wear. And why worry about your clothing? Look at the lilies of the field and how they grow. They don't work or make their clothing" (Matthew 6:25,28).

God cares about his beautiful creation. That's why he made Adam and Eve the first care takers of the earth. But God cares for people even more than flowers.

Sometimes we fuss and worry about things in our lives, but if we remember how much God loves and cares for us, we can be assured that he will give us everything we need.

The next time you are tempted to worry, consider the lilies. What is something you could do instead of worrying?

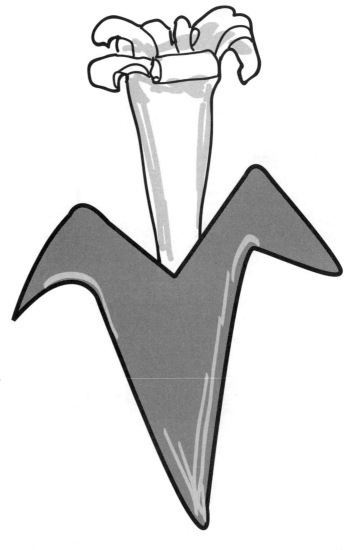

What To Do

1. Cut paper into an 8x8-inch square.
2. Starting at one corner, roll the square into a cone shape and tape the seam at the top and bottom.
3. Cut off the top of the cone so that it is even.
4. Make six 2-inch slits around the top of the cone.
5. Use a pencil to curl the six sections down; curl the section around a pencil tightly, hold for a few seconds, and then remove the pencil.
6. Use the pattern to trace and cut a set of leaves from green construction paper.
7. Write the memory verse on the leaves.

Lily Leaves

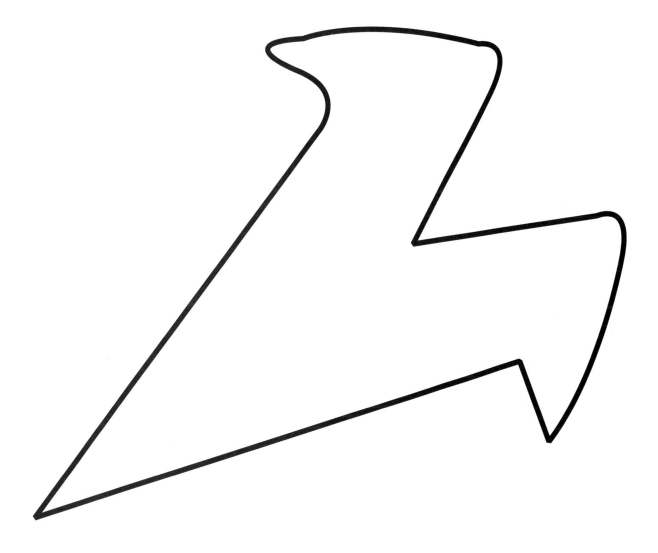

Seeds Bring Forth Life

I tell you the truth, unless a kernel of wheat is planted in the soil and dies, it remains alone. But its death will produce many new kernels—a plentiful harvest of new lives. **John 12:24**

What It's All About

Have you ever planted a seed and watched it grow? Seeds seem small, but with soil, rain, and sun, they grow into plants. Unless a seed is planted, it will not grow and produce. Jesus' death was like a seed that was buried and rose from the earth to bring forth new life. Jesus paid the price for our sins. Because of this, we can have new life in him. Color the picture and draw a beautiful flower growing out of the pot.

Earth Day Word Search

The highest heavens and the earth and everything in it all belong to the LORD your God. **Deuteronomy 10:14**

What It's All About

When God created the Earth, he also created humans to care for his creation. Everything on Earth belongs to God, so it's our responsibility to take good care of it. On Earth Day, many countries around the world make an extra effort to care for the planet. What are some things that you can do to celebrate Earth Day? Some ideas might be to plant trees or flowers, make your own paper, learn about recycling, or clean up litter in a public park. Even small changes make a big difference.

Find the words in the box that are hidden in the square.

```
J N G V B G O G R E E N L X G
V T Y M F A T E R E C Y C L E
A O C P L A N E T O U I Z F U
S N A T U R E X T Q X U V I H
E W T U N J B O J V Z Q E X O
Z K R A E N E R G Y V W O Y N
V V E F N T F F U T G C M N M
G L E A B E R T N X D O X Q A
C X E Y N N A E O I V M Q N C
Q C P R O T E C T H W P G O I
O V M B Y C W A T E R O Z N K
F O Z S U A I R Z Z J S G R X
K F T D D Y A L E V R T R N W
U R E U S E P E D C W B D F I
R R A B S D G Y R G I X C B W
```

Word Box

air, compost, energy, green, nature, protect, recycle, reuse, tree, water

Caretakers of the Earth

The highest heavens and the earth and everything in it all belong to the Lord your God. **Deuteronomy 10:14**

What It's All About

God created a beautiful world for us to live in. He filled it with colorful plants, amazing creatures, bright stars, and deep waters. Out of all of God's creation, humans are his favorite. That's why he made Adam and Eve the first caretakers of the Garden of Eden.

Earth Day reminds us to care for our planet. It was first celebrated on April 22, 1970. It is a day that brings awareness about environmental issues. Caring for the earth can be as easy as learning to recycle, composting, or switching to reusable items.

Color the picture as a reminder that we should all do our part to keep the planet clean.

New Life in Christ

My old self has been crucified with Christ. It is no longer I who live, but Christ lives in me. So I live in this earthly body by trusting in the Son of God, who loved me and gave himself for me. **Galatians 2:20**

What It's All About

Jesus came to Earth as a baby, just like you and me. Jesus died so that we can be forgiven of our sins and someday live with him forever in Heaven. While we are here on Earth, we are to care for it and all of God's creation.

Color the picture, thank Jesus for his death on the cross, and ask him to help you follow him while you are living on the Earth God gave us.

Teacher Day Celebration

The Lord says, "I will guide you along the best pathway for your life. I will advise you and watch over you. **Psalm 32:8**

What It's All About

A good teacher's mission is to see their students succeed. They try hard to make learning fun, but sometimes they feel like their hard work goes unnoticed. Let's make a special effort this year to make our teachers feel special. Color the picture on this sheet as a reminder to do one or more of the listed activities for your teacher.

> Homeschooled children can celebrate this day by honoring their parent or guardian with these activities.

What to Do

Plan acts of kindness and appreciation for your teachers.

Teacher Survey

Ask your teacher to fill out a list of questions about themselves and the things that they like. Ask about their favorite book, movie, or restaurant, or ask to describe their dream classroom. Buy or make gifts for your teachers based on their answers. They'll appreciate your thoughtfulness.

Teacher Awards

- Scissors • Yellow and blue construction paper
- Ruler • Paper plate • Crayons or markers • Glue

1. Cut out a large circle from yellow construction paper approximately the same size as the center of the paper plate.
2. Cut out two 2x8-inch rectangles from blue construction paper.
3. Glue the yellow circle to the center of the paper plate.
4. Glue the blue rectangles to the back of the paper plate so that they extend past the edge of the plate like award ribbons.
5. Cut slits about ½ inch apart around the edge of the plate.
6. On the yellow circle, write the best thing about your teacher, a happy memory, a thankful note, or draw a picture of them.
7. Give it to your teacher to show your thanks.

Thankful Photo Album

Children draw posters that show their thanks for their teacher. Present the posters to the teachers. Optional: Take pictures of each child with their poster. Print out the pictures and put them in a photo album. Give the album to the teacher to show the class's appreciation.

Community Help

Children can have bake sales, car washes, sell their used toys, or donate their allowance to raise money for Teacher Appreciation Day. Use the money to refurbish the teachers' lounge, restock the craft supply closet, buy them a new coffee maker or gift cards, and more!

Thank You, Teacher

Direct your children onto the right path, and when they are older, they will not leave it. **Proverbs 22:6**

What It's All About

Have you ever wondered how craft materials, decorations, or game supplies magically appear in your classroom? Your teacher does a lot of behind-the-scenes work to prepare for your lessons. You can show your teacher how much you care by drawing a picture of the two of you below. Then, write a note describing your favorite things about them, a special memory, or an acrostic poem with their name. Give it to your teacher to show your appreciation.

Thank you for all that you do!

Teacher Feature

Students are not greater than their teacher. But the student who is fully trained will become like the teacher. **Luke 6:40**

What It's All About

Teacher Appreciation Day is the best time to let your teacher know how much you care. Teachers work very hard to make sure your lessons are fun and memorable.

Draw a picture of your teacher below. Above the picture, write a quote or a fun memory you have with them.

178 • Teacher Appreciation Day

Coupon Book of Promises

Reward her for all she has done. Let her deeds publicly declare her praise. **Proverbs 31:31**

What You Need

• Crayons or markers • Index cards • Colored construction paper • Scissors • Stapler

Preparation

Photocopy this page, making one for each child.

What It's All About

Mothers or guardians help you do things all day long. When you were little, they helped you learn to walk, eat nicely, use the toilet, use your manners, and more. You might still get reminders from them to do your chores or clean up after yourself. It is a lot of work to take care of a family, and your mom or guardian would love for you to be a cheerful helper. Today, we'll make a Coupon Book of Promises where you can make goals to be a super helper. Color this picture as a reminder to make good on your coupons.

What To Do

1. Trace the index card on colored construction paper twice. These will be your front and back covers.
2. Cut the rectangles out.
3. On one write "For Mom" or the name of whoever you're making the card for. On the other, write the memory verse.
4. On the index cards, write or draw something you promise to do for your mother. Some suggestions include: one cheerful dish washing, one thorough room cleaning, one laundry helper, or running one errand.
5. Give the coupon book to your mother or guardian on Mother's Day. They can tear out and redeem the coupons as things need to be done. Even if your biological mother is not in your life, your father or guardian will be happy to celebrate Mother's Day with you. They will understand that you are recognizing that you care for them like a mother would.

I Love My Mom Card

Honor your father and mother. Then you will live a long, full life in the land the LORD your God is giving you. **Exodus 20:12**

What You Need
- Crayons or markers • Scissors

Preparation
Photocopy this page, making a copy for each child.

What It's All About
Mother's Day is a day to show your mom how much you care. It is a lot of work to take care of a family's needs, but moms try their best to care for everyone. Many people give their mothers flowers, cards, or candies as a sign of their love. Today, you get to make your own special card.

What To Do
1. Connect the dots and then color in the letters.
2. Cut out the card and fold the paper in half.
3. On the inside, write a sweet note to your mom. Get creative! Draw a picture of you two together. Write a thank-you note, or write words that describe her. Let her know how much you care about her.

Mother's Day Poem

So give your father and mother joy! May she who gave you birth be happy. **Proverbs 23:25**

What You Need
- Crayons or markers

Preparation
Photocopy this page, making one for each child.

What It's All About
Moms are very special people. A good mom takes care of your needs and cares about your feelings. She comforts you when you are sad, or reads you bedtime stories, or teaches your new things. Today, you can show your mom how much you care with a poem and a picture.

What To Do
Choose words from the box to fill the blanks. Then, draw your mother or guardian in the flower heart. Write their name on the banner and color in the flowers.

On Mother's Day, I tell you,

I'm just as good as _____;

I try to mind my manners

And do as I am _____.

I give my mom a present

And help around the _____;

And when she says, "Be quiet,"

You'd think I was a _____.

I tell her that I love her

And sometimes give her _____.

I say, "I think you're pretty,

And I'm very glad you're _____."

Then Mom will say at evening,

"It's Mother's Day, that's _____,

wish that we could celebrate

Every day next _____!"

clear	mouse
flowers	ours
gold	told
house	year

Bible Mothers Quiz

Children, obey your parents because you belong to the Lord, for this is the right thing to do. **Ephesians 6:1**

What You Need
- Bibles • Crayons or markers

Preparation
Photocopy this page, making one for each child.

What It's All About
People have known the importance of honoring mothers, even before Mother's Day was an official holiday. For example, in medieval England, young people who worked as servants honored their mothers by bringing flowers or sweet cakes home. In the United States, Mother's Day became an official holiday in 1914. Traditionally, a red carnation was worn to honor living mothers and a white carnation was worn in remembrance of mothers who are no longer living. Even in Bible times, people knew to honor their mothers (Proverbs 23:25). Today, let's test your knowledge on mothers mentioned in the Bible.

What to Do
Answer the questions about these mothers mentioned in the Bible. If you don't know their name, it's OK to write "mother of (insert child's name)." See if your answer is correct by looking up the Bible reference.

1. What mother hid her baby in a tiny basket boat? (Exodus 6:20) _____

2. What mother went to a wedding feast and asked her son to help? (John 2:1) _____

3. What mother prayed for a baby boy and when he was older took him to live and work in the Tabernacle? (1 Samuel 1:10–11, 20) _____

4. What mother married Isaac and had twin sons? (Genesis 24:51) _____

5. Who was the first mother? (Genesis 3:20) _____

6. What mother had a son who preached in the wilderness? (Luke 1:13) _____

7. What mother had a son whom his brothers sold to be a slave in Egypt? (Genesis 29:20) _____

8. What mother laughed when she heard she would have a child? (Genesis 21:1) _____

9. What mother gave Abraham his first son? (Genesis 16:15) _____

10. Which mother gave birth to a king who later built the Jewish Temple? (2 Samuel 12:24) _____

Alternate Idea
Number ten index cards and attach them to a wall. Children divide into teams. The first player of each team gets a chance to throw a ball at the wall. If the ball hits an index card, ask the team the corresponding question. If they get it right, hand the team the index card. If they get the question wrong, the next team gets a chance to answer it. Continue to play until all the index cards have been hit. The team with the most index cards recites the memory verse.

Mothers Are God's Masterpiece

For we are God's masterpiece. He has created us anew in Christ Jesus, so we can do the good things he planned for us long ago. **Ephesians 2:10**

What It's All About

Ephesians 2:10 says we are God's masterpiece. That means we are highly valued. Mothers are some of God's most special masterpieces. Some mothers are given to us at birth, some through adoption, and sometimes God brings other people into our lives to be our guardian and care for us the way a mother would. Name one thing your mother or guardian does for you for which you can thank her.

Color this picture and place it in your room as a reminder to thank your mother often.

Mother's Day • 183

Sarah Was a Woman of Faith

It was by faith that even Sarah was able to have a child, though she was barren and was too old. She believed that God would keep his promise. **Hebrews 11:11**

What It's All About

Sarah was Abraham's wife. Abraham and Sarah both wanted a child very badly. God promised that he would give them a son, and he did. However, it took a long time for that to happen. When Sarah finally gave birth to Isaac, she was deeply devoted to taking care of him. Sarah and her family did not live in a house like we do. They lived in a tent. How different would your life be if you lived in a tent?

Draw pots, jars, and baskets in the tent. Color the rest of the picture.

Mother of Faith

When she speaks, her words are wise, and she gives instructions with kindness. **Proverbs 31:26**

What It's All About

The Bible tells us that nothing was more important in Eunice's life than the early training of her son, Timothy (2 Timothy 1:5). Grandmother Lois assisted her in raising Timothy to be an unselfish man who was loyally devoted to Christ. This was very important because when Timothy grew up, he traveled with Paul on many of his missionary journeys. Nothing is more important than for a mother to raise her children to serve God. Thank God for the mother that he has given you. Honor her in everything you do.

Color this picture as a reminder of Eunice, Lois, and other biblical mothers.

Grocery Store Helper

She carefully watches everything in her household and suffers nothing from laziness. **Proverbs 31:27**

What It's All About

God tells us to honor our mothers. We can honor our mothers and guardians by being obedient, loving, and helpful.

Draw groceries in the shopping cart and color the rest of the picture as a reminder to tell your mother or guardian that you love them.

186 • Mother's Day

Jochebed, Miriam, and Moses

Let me hear of your unfailing love each morning, for I am trusting you. Show me where to walk, for I give myself to you. **Psalm 143:8**

What It's All About

Does your mother take good care of you? Moses' mother, Jochebed, was a courageous mother who trusted God. When Pharaoh ordered all of the Hebrew boy babies to be killed, Jochebed placed baby Moses in a basket. She put it in the river, hoping that God would see to his safety. Miriam followed the basket and watched as Pharaoh's daughter found the baby. She wanted to adopt him. Miriam suggested that the princess hire Jochebed to care for Moses until he was old enough to stay in the palace. The princess agreed. What a miracle!

Color this picture as a reminder of ways your mother or guardian takes care of you.

Flowers for Mother

Don't neglect your mother's instruction. **Proverbs 1:8**

What It's All About

The Bible makes it clear that you are to honor your mother. Sometimes that is hard to do. When you honor your mother or guardian, you are showing your love for God and for them.

Color the picture and give it to your mother or guardian. Write a thank you note on the blank lines.

_____

_____

_____

Happy Mother's Day

Her children stand and bless her. Her husband praises her. **Proverbs 31:28**

What You Need
- Loving Gardener (p. 190) • Crayons or markers

What to Do
Photocopy this page and Loving Gardener, making one of each page for each child.

What It's All About
Even if your mother or guardian does not grow a garden, they are still growing something very precious. They are growing you! Just like a gardener who makes sure the plants have the proper care, your mother or guardian sees that you get proper care. Can you think of some ways that your mother or guardian makes sure you grow up big and strong?

Color this page. On the Loving Gardener page, draw a picture of yourself on the inside of the flower and give the sheet to your mother or guardian.

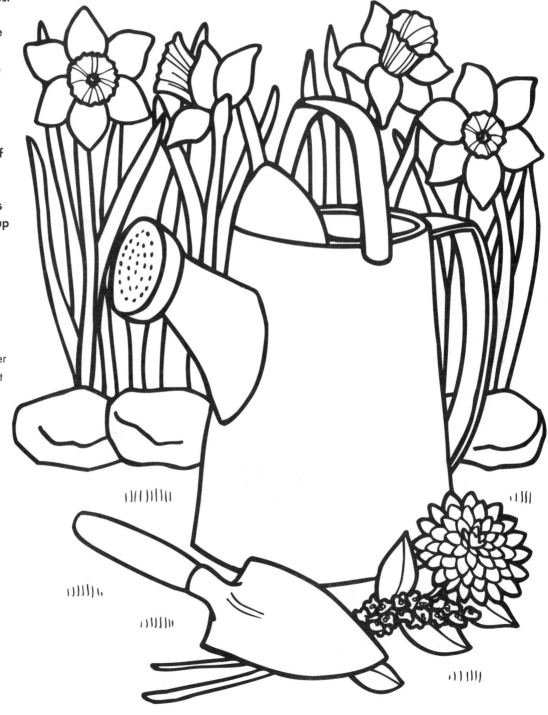

Mother's Day • 189

© 2021 Rose Publishing, LLC. Permission to photocopy granted to original purchaser only. *The Super-Sized Book of Holidays, Special Days, & Celebrations.*

Loving Gardener

To: _____

From: _____

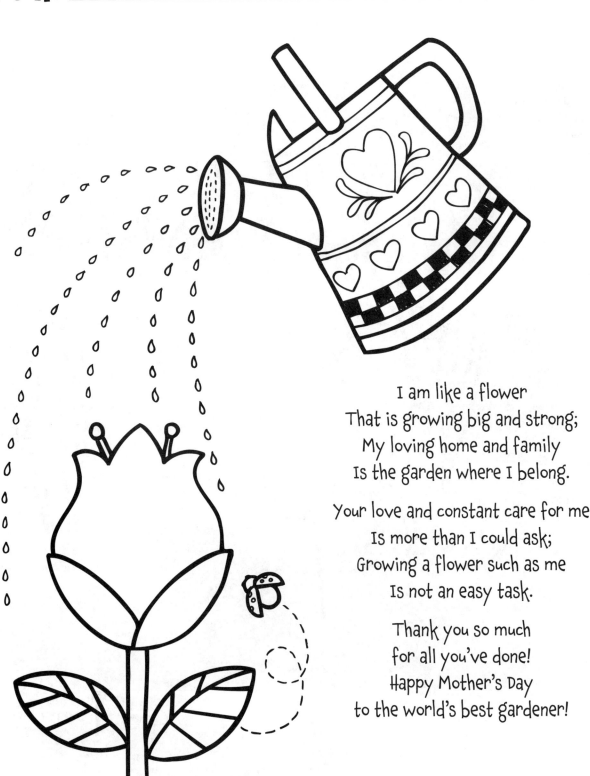

I am like a flower
That is growing big and strong;
My loving home and family
Is the garden where I belong.

Your love and constant care for me
Is more than I could ask;
Growing a flower such as me
Is not an easy task.

Thank you so much
for all you've done!
Happy Mother's Day
to the world's best gardener!

Mother's Arms

I will comfort you there in Jerusalem as a mother comforts her child. **Isaiah 66:13**

What You Need
- Full of Love (p. 192) • Crayons or markers

What to Do
Photocopy this page and Full of Love, making one of each page for each child.

What It's All About
Have you ever been frightened by a terrible storm? Who was there to make you feel safe? Just being in the arms of someone who loves you is such a comfort at times when you need it. The Bible tells us that God is like a mother who comforts us in frightening moments. He protects us and keeps us safe. We need to thank our mothers and guardians for the protection and safety they give us.

Color this picture. Then color Full of Love and give it to your mother or guardian.

Mother's Day • 191

Full of Love

To: _____

From: _____

A Royal Birthday

See how very much our Father loves us, for he calls us his children, and that is what we are! **1 John 3:1**

What It's All About

Victoria Day is a Canadian holiday that celebrates Queen Victoria's birthday. She ruled for about sixty-three and a half years, making her one of the longest reigning monarchs! When she died in 1901, Canada made her birthday an official holiday. Many celebrate by having picnics, parades, fireworks, and sports games. On her birthday, we can also remember that we are children of royalty because God is the true king, and his reign never ends.

Color the picture.

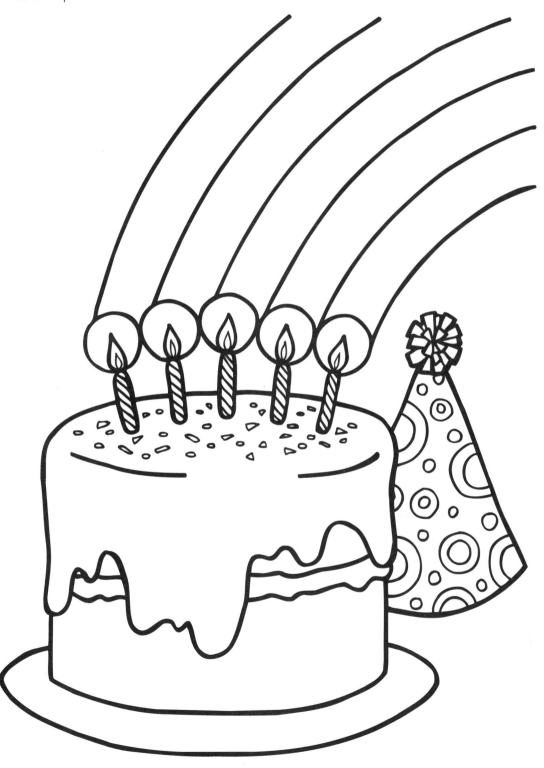

Victoria Day • 193

Medal of Peace

God blesses those who work for peace, for they will be called the children of God. **Matthew 5:9**

What You Need

• Crayons or markers • Circular object • Construction paper • Scissors • Glue • Lightweight cardboard
• Decorative materials (gold star stickers, ribbons, glitter, etc.) • Tape • Safety pins, one for each child

What It's All About

Memorial Day is a special day to honor soldiers who have died to protect our country. Many people honor soldiers by decorating their tombstones with flowers or small American flags. One of the best ways to honor these soldiers is to learn peaceful ways to settle arguments. What are some ways we could do that?

There are many ways to be heroic other than fighting in wars. Can you think of any? Some examples might be speaking up for what is right, not following friends' ideas to break rules, or making friends with new kids who are different from you.

A hero is someone who puts others' needs before their own. Jesus is the greatest example of a heroic sacrifice. He died on the cross for our sins so that we can live forever with him.

As we celebrate Memorial Day this year, let's remember that those who work for peace will be called children of God. Today we'll make hero medals for each everyone to wear as a reminder to be an peacemaker.

What To Do

1. Trace circular object onto construction paper, making one for each medal.
2. Cut out the circles.
3. Glue the circles on lightweight cardboard. Cut out.
4. Decorate the medals with decorative materials and colorful designs. Get creative by drawing symbols of peace like a dove, an olive branch, or a lion and lamb together.
5. Tape or glue a safety pin to the back.
6. Pin the medal to your shirt.

Prodigal Son Story

Honor your father and mother. Then you will live a long, full life in the land the Lord your God is giving you. **Exodus 20:12**

What It's All About

There is a story in the Bible about a rebellious young man who wanted his father to give him his inheritance. The son wanted to leave home and live on his own. It must have broken the father's heart to let his son go, because he loved his son very much.

When all of the boy's money was gone and he had nothing to eat, he returned home. When his father saw him coming, his father ran to meet him and welcome the boy home, forgiving him for all he had done.

Have you ever done something for which you had to go to your dad or guardian and ask forgiveness? Your father or guardian loves you so much that they will forgive you. When he does punish you, it is to help correct you so that you grow up to be responsible.

Our heavenly Father is much like our earthly fathers in that way. When we do something that does not please him, we can ask forgiveness, and he will forgive us. He loves us more than we can imagine. He gave us our earthly fathers and guardians to teach us his ways. Honor the father or guardian that God has given you.

As part of our Father's Day celebration, let's color this picture to remember this story about a father's love. Write answers to the questions on the lines provided.

Discussion Questions

1. How did the father feel when his son left home?

_____

_____

2. Why do our fathers sometimes punish us?

_____

_____

3. Why should we honor our earthly fathers?

_____

_____

I Love My Dad Card

I will be your Father, and you will be my sons and daughters, says the LORD Almighty. **2 Corinthians 6:18**

What You Need
- Crayons or markers • Scissors

Preparation
Photocopy this page, making a copy for each child.

What It's All About
Father's Day is a day to show your dad or guardian how much you care. It is a lot of work to take care of a family's needs, but dads and guardians try their best to care for everyone. Sometimes, your biological father might not be that person. But there is someone, and it could be a woman, who God gave you to act like a father in your life. Today, you get to make a special card for that person.

What To Do
1. Connect the dots and then color in the letters.
2. Cut out the card and fold the paper in half.
3. On the inside, write a sweet note to your father. Get creative! Draw a picture of you two together. Write a thank-you note or write words that describe them. Let them know how much you care about them. Don't worry that the card says "Dad," if you don't have a dad in your life. Whoever takes care of you will understand you're saying that they are like a father to you.

196 • Father's Day

© 2021 Rose Publishing, LLC. Permission to photocopy granted to original purchaser only. *The Super-Sized Book of Holidays, Special Days, & Celebrations.*

Dad's Key Rack

Honor your father and mother. Then you will live a long, full life in the land the LORD your God is giving you. **Exodus 20:12**

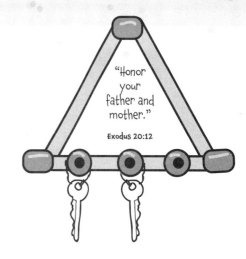

What You Need

- Markers • Poster board • Scissors • Ruler • Glue
- Craft sticks, three for each child • Wooden beads
- Soda can tab, one for each child

Preparation

Photocopy this page, making one for each child.

What It's All About

Father's Day is a special day to thank your father or guardian for all the hard work they do to care for you and your family. Our memory verse talks about honoring your parents. This means showing parents and guardians respect and to listening when they ask you to do something. Today, you will make a gift to celebrate your father or whoever acts like a father to you—whether it's your mother, guardian, or other caring family member.

What To Do

1. Trace the triangle pattern onto poster board and cut it out.
2. Write the memory verse in the center of the poster board triangle with a marker.
3. Glue a craft stick to each of the three outside edges.
4. Glue one wooden bead to each corner of the triangle and three wooden beads across the bottom facing out (for key pegs).
5. Glue the soda can tab to the back of the triangle for a hanger.

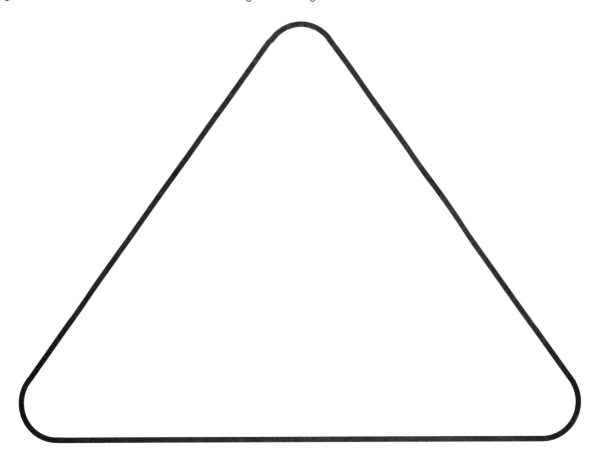

Father's Day

Bible Fathers Quiz

Fathers, do not provoke your children to anger by the way you treat them. Rather, bring them up with the discipline and instruction that comes from the Lord. **Ephesians 6:4**

What You Need
- Bibles • Crayons or markers

Preparation
Photocopy this page, making one for each child.

What It's All About
Father's Day began in 1924 as a day to honor fathers. Originally, a red rose was worn to honor living fathers, and a white rose was worn to remember fathers who are no longer living. Father's Day provides an opportunity for children to learn the importance of honoring and obeying their fathers or guardians.

What to Do
Answer the questions about these fathers mentioned in the Bible. If you don't know their name, it's OK to write "father of (insert child's name)."

See if your answer is correct by looking up the Bible reference.

1. What father built the great Temple in Jerusalem? (1 Kings 8:22,29–30) _____

2. What father had two fishermen sons who became Jesus' followers? (Matthew 4:21) _____

3. What man was called the father of his people? (Genesis 18:18) _____

4. What father came to Jesus that he might heal his sick daughter? (Luke 8:41) _____

5. What father had twin sons and was deceived by one of them? (Genesis 27:22) _____

6. What father became speechless until his son was born? (Luke 1:13) _____

7. What father was the first sailor? (Genesis 6:9) _____

8. What father went from sling to throne? (2 Samuel 5:25) _____

9. Who was the first father? (Genesis 3:20) _____

10. Which father was a carpenter from Nazareth? (Luke 2:4) _____

Alternate Idea
Number ten index cards and attach them to a wall. Children divide into teams. The first player of each team gets a chance to throw a ball at the wall. If the ball hits an index card, ask the team the corresponding question. If they get it right, hand the team the index card. If they get the question wrong, the next team gets a chance to answer it. Continue to play until all the index cards have been hit. The team with the most index cards recites the memory verse.

Heavenly Father Crossword

The LORD is like a father to his children, tender and compassionate to those who fear him. **Psalm 103:13**

What You Need
- Crayons or markers

Preparation
Photocopy this page, making one for each child.

What It's All About

Your Father in Heaven loves and cares for you just like good fathers on Earth do. When you become a Christian you are adopted into God's family and you become his child. Psalm 103:13 says that God is compassionate toward those who fear him. In this context, *to fear God* means to honor him. You can honor him by respecting those around you and obeying your parents.

Fill in the crossword using the verse words in the gray box. Hint: Count the number of letters in each word, and then fill in the longest word first.

Word Box

CHILDREN
COMPASSIONATE
FATHER
FEAR
LIKE
LORD
TENDER
WHO

Father's Day • 199

© 2021 Rose Publishing, LLC. Permission to photocopy granted to original purchaser only. *The Super-Sized Book of Holidays, Special Days, & Celebrations.*

We Are Children of God

Since we are his children, we are his heirs. In fact, together with Christ we are heirs of God's glory. But if we are to share his glory, we must also share his suffering. **Romans 8:17**

What It's All About

When you become a Christian, you become God's child. God is your heavenly Father. You are heirs of God and co-heirs with Jesus. Being an heir means you become part of God's family and you share in the great treasures that he has planned for you.

Color this picture as a reminder that all kinds of treasures are waiting in Heaven for you!

Adopted into God's Family

So you have not received a spirit that makes you fearful slaves. Instead, you received God's Spirit when he adopted you as his own children. Now we call him, "Abba, Father." **Romans 8:15**

What It's All About

The Bible says we are adopted into God's family when we become believers in Jesus. When a child is adopted, they get a new family. God adopts us into his family, and he loves and accepts us.

Write your name and today's date on the lines, draw your face on the child, color, and decorate the certificate.

Jesus and His Father Joseph

Jesus grew in wisdom and in stature and in favor with God and all the people. **Luke 2:52**

What It's All About

Jesus grew up in a small town called Nazareth where he helped his earthly father, Joseph, a carpenter. Jesus was called the carpenter's son. He learned from his father how to make things out of wood. Your father or guardian can teach you many things but you have to be patient and willing to learn.

Color the picture of Jesus helping Joseph.

Adam Tells His Son about God

My children, listen when your father corrects you. Pay attention and learn good judgment. **Proverbs 4:1**

What It's All About

Before the Bible was written, children learned about God from their parents. Imagine how exciting it was for Adam, the first man, to teach his children about God. Adam walked and talked with God in the beautiful Garden of Eden. Fathers like Adam teach valuable lessons from their own experiences so their children know how to live a life pleasing to God.

Color the picture.

Father's Day • 203

Teaching about God

Teach [Bible verses] to your children. Talk about them when you are at home and when you are on the road, when you are going to bed and when you are getting up. **Deuteronomy 11:19**

What It's All About

Until you learned to read, someone else had to read Bible stories to you. You are lucky to live in a time when you can freely read the Bible. Long ago, people did not have the Bible. Parents taught their children the stories that their parents had taught them. Today, your parents and guardians can teach you, but they have the Bible to use.

Draw a cover on the Bible and flowers in the vase. Then, color the picture.

204 • Father's Day

Abraham's Big Family

A whole nation came from this one man who was as good as dead—a nation with so many people that, like the stars in the sky and the sand on the seashore, there is no way to count them. **Hebrews 11:12**

What It's All About

Have you ever sang the song "Father Abraham Had Many Sons"? Abraham is considered the father of the Jewish people because God promised that through his family there would be many children—too many to count! Abraham's descendants are his children, grandchildren, great-grandchildren, and so on. But most importantly, God promised that a Savior would eventually be born in Abraham's family line. Many years later, Jesus was born, just as God promised. If we believe in Jesus, we can be part of that family, too! Color the picture of Abraham. Draw faces around him to show God's big family.

Father's Day • 205

We Are Abraham's Family

[God told Abraham,] *"I will multiply your descendants until they become as numerous as the sands along the seashore—too many to count."* **Genesis 32:12**

What It's All About

Have you ever scooped up a handful of sand on the beach and tired to count each tiny grain? It's impossible because there are just too many! God told Abraham that his family would grow to the number of sand grains on the seashore! Because Jesus came to save all people from their sins, Christians also are considered part of Abraham's family. So when you hear that Father Abraham had many sons (and daughters), if you are a Christian, you are one of them, too.

Draw your family of believers on the beach and color the picture.

Happy Father's Day

Seek [God's] will in all you do, and he will show you which path to take. **Proverbs 3:6**

What You Need
- Father's Day Card (p. 208) • Crayons or markers

Preparation
Photocopy this page and Father's Day Card, making one for each child.

What It's All About

Have you ever gone hiking with people who led you through the mountain paths because they knew the way? God is like a guide. He can help you make the right decisions. Your father or guardian has a lot of wisdom to keep you from going on the wrong path. Our Heavenly Father will also guide us if we obey him and follow his commands.

Color the picture below as a reminder of how God guides us. On the Father's Day Card page, draw a picture of yourself in the frame and give the sheet to your father.

Father's Day • 207

Father's Day Card

To: _____

From: _____

I hope I make you proud of me
By the things I say and do;
And on this happy Father's Day
Comes a great big "I love you!"

Happy Father's Day from one of your biggest fans!

Father's Wisdom

A house is built by wisdom and becomes strong through good sense. **Proverbs 24:3**

What You Need
- Father's Day Wish (p. 210) • Crayons or markers

Preparation
Photocopy Father's Day Wish, making one for each child.

What It's All About
Some dads or guardians know how to do many things around the house, such as fix a leaky faucet or repair a broken window. Some even build their family's houses. The Bible says that wisdom and understanding are what make a strong household. Wisdom and understanding come from knowing God and his Word.

Color the tools and draw your father or guardian and you in the center of the tools. Draw additional balloons on the Father's Day Wish page and color it. Give it to your father or guardian.

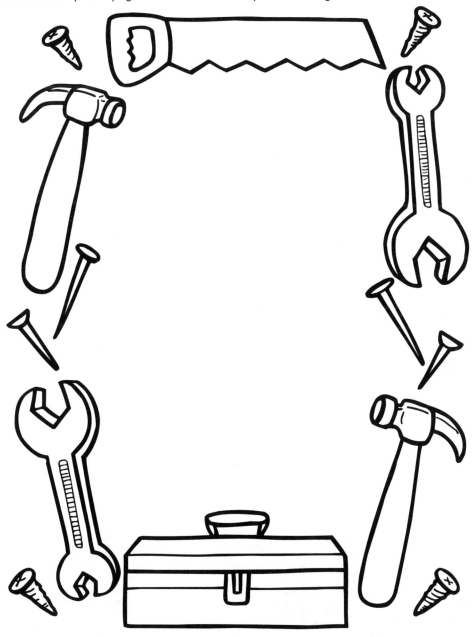

Father's Day • 209

Father's Day Wish

To: _____

From: _____

Wishing you the very best Father's Day for the very best father!

Juneteenth Prayer Chain

There is no longer Jew or Gentile, slave or free, male and female. For you are all one in Christ Jesus. **Galatians 3:28**

What You Need

- Scissors • Colored construction paper • Dark colored markers • Tape

What It's All About

Juneteenth celebrates the end of slavery in the United States of America. Abraham Lincoln ended slavery during the Civil War, but it took two years for the new laws to be enforced in Texas. On June 19, 1865 enslaved people in Texas finally received their freedom. Many African-American families celebrate Juneteenth with barbecues, big family picnics, and games. As Christians, we can celebrate our freedom from sin because of Jesus' death on the cross. We are no longer slaves to sin; instead, we are free children of God.

What To Do

1. Cut paper into approximately 1x8-inch strips.
2. On each strip write a prayer or the name of someone you'd like to pray for. Remember to pray for your teachers, government leaders, country, and planet, too.
3. Take one strip and tape the ends together. It's your first chain.
4. Slip your next strip through the chain. Tape the ends of the strip together. Now the chains are linked.
5. Continue this way until all your chains are linked.
6. Put the prayer chain near your bed as a reminder to pray.

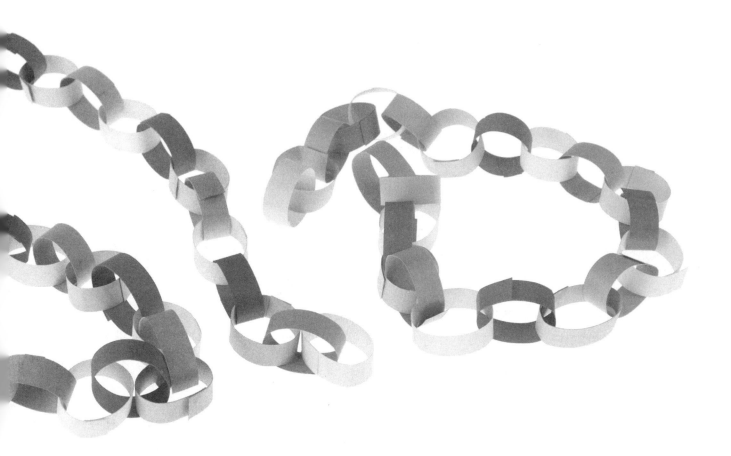

Code of Chains

Now you are free from your slavery to sin, and you have become slaves to righteous living. **Romans 6:18**

What You Need
- Crayons or markers

Preparation
Photocopy this page, making one for each child.

What It's All About
Juneteenth, also known as Freedom Day, celebrates the end of slavery in the United States of America. It was first celebrated on June 19, 1865, when slaves in Texas learned of their freedom. Our memory verse talks about being set free from our slavery to sin. Anyone who believes in Jesus has been set free from sin. This means that if you do anything wrong, you can ask God (and the people you hurt) for forgiveness, and you will be freed.

What To Do
Complete the code to find out what it means to be slaves to righteous living. Match the number below a blank with the same number on a link in the chain and write the link's letter in the blank.

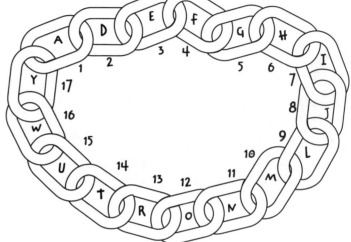

__ __ __ __ __ C __ __ __ __ __
4 15 9 9 17   12 10 10 7 14

__ __ __ __ S __ __ __ __ __ __ __ __
17 12 15 13   3 9 4   14 12   5 12 2

S __ __ __ C __ __ __ __ __ __ __
  12   6 3   1 11   5 15 7 2 3

__ __ __ __ __ __ __ __ __ __
17 12 15 14 12   1   5 12 12 2

__ __ __ __.
 9 7 4 3

Fashionable Flags

May we shout for joy when we hear of your victory and raise a victory banner in the name of our God. **Psalm 20:5**

What You Need

- Flag Patterns (p. 214) • Card stock • Dark colored markers • Scissors • White, blue, and red felt
- Hot glue gun • ¼x12-inch dowel rods • Paper • White beads or star stickers

Tip

If felt is not available, use colored construction paper.

Preparation

Photocopy Flag Patterns onto card stock, making one for every three children. These will be shared as tracing templates.

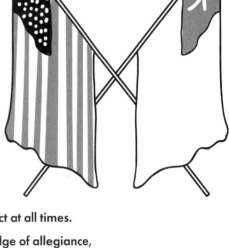

What It's All About

Our flag is a symbol of our nation. We love our nation and are proud of it. We fly our flag at government offices, schools, churches, and many homes and businesses. When the flag passes by in a parade, people stand to their feet, men remove their hats, people place their hands over their hearts, and servicemen and women raise their hands in salute and stand at attention.

The flag should never be dragged on the ground and cannot be used as a tablecloth or clothing. It must be shown respect at all times.

The Christian flag stands for the kingdom of God on Earth. It has a pledge of allegiance, just as our national flag. The pledge to the Christian flag goes like this:

"I pledge allegiance to the Christian flag, and to the Savior for whose kingdom it stands; one Savior, crucified, risen, and coming again with life and liberty to all who believe."

Today, we get to make our own American and Christian flags.

What To Do to Make a Christian Flag

1. Trace the rectangle pattern onto white felt, the square pattern onto blue felt, and the cross pattern onto red felt.
2. Cut out the shapes.
3. On the white rectangle, apply glue along the ½-inch edge.
4. Roll up the dowel rod in the white felt for a flag pole.
5. Glue the red cross onto the center of the blue square.
6. Glue the blue square onto the upper left corner of the white rectangle.
7. Write the memory verse on a small piece of paper and glue it to the back of the flag.

What To Do to Make an American Flag

1. Trace the rectangle pattern onto white felt and the square pattern onto blue felt.
2. Cut out the shapes.
3. On the white rectangle, apply glue along the ½-inch edge.
4. Roll up the dowel rod in the white felt for a flag pole.
5. Cut out five ½x5 ½-inch strips of red felt.
6. Space the red strips evenly apart on the white felt and glue in place.
7. Glue the blue square to the top left corner the white felt.
8. To add stars on the blue square, glue on white beads or star stickers.

> This activity can also be used on Flag Day, which is celebrated on June 14 and commemorates the adoption of the USA flag.

Independence Day • 213

Flag Patterns

214 • Independence Day

Firework Rockets

[The disciples] were all filled with the Holy Spirit. Then they preached the word of God with boldness. **Acts 4:31**

What You Need

- Paper-towel or toilet-paper tubes, one for each child • Blue, red, and white construction paper
- Scissors • Glue • Tape • Markers • Decorative materials (gold star stickers, ribbons, pipe cleaners, glitter, etc.)

What It's All About

Independence Day reminds us of the signing of the Declaration of Independence on July 4, 1776. This date marks the birthday of the United States of America. When we think of America, we think of a land of freedom. But America will only be free as long as its people look to Christ for leadership and guidance. We celebrate that freedom on the Fourth of July.

July 4th is often celebrated with fireworks, so we'll each get to make a rocket. Like the rocket which contains explosive powder, we can be filled with the Holy Spirit and receive much more power than fireworks have. Also, fireworks explode and their power is gone as the sparks die falling to the ground. The power we receive from Jesus through the Holy Spirit will not die. The Holy Spirit will see us through all that life has to offer and then be with us in Heaven.

What To Do

1. Wrap a piece of construction paper around the paper-towel or toilet-paper tube, covering it completely.
2. Cut off excess paper.
3. Glue the paper to the tube.
4. Cut a circle from construction paper that is an inch or so larger than the opening of the tube.
5. Cut a slit to the center of the circle and bend it around to make a cone.
6. Tape the cone together.
7. Glue the cone to the end of the tube.
8. Decorate the rocket with markers and other decorative materials.
9. Print on the rocket, "Filled with the power of God."

Celebration Crossword

For the Lord is the Spirit, and wherever the Spirit of the Lord is, there is freedom. **2 Corinthians 3:17**

What You Need
- Crayons or markers

Preparation
Photocopy this page, making one for each child.

What It's All About
The Fourth of July is much more than just parades, picnics, and fireworks. The first Americans declared their independence from England on July fourth and were free to pursue a better way of life. They were no longer bound to the laws and regulations of another country. Not only can we celebrate our country's freedom, but we can also celebrate our freedom from sin because of Jesus' sacrifice on the cross. Every day is Independence Day for Christians.

What To Do
Fill in the crossword boxes with the words from the gray box. Tip: Start by counting the letters of each word and inserting the longest one into the crossword first.

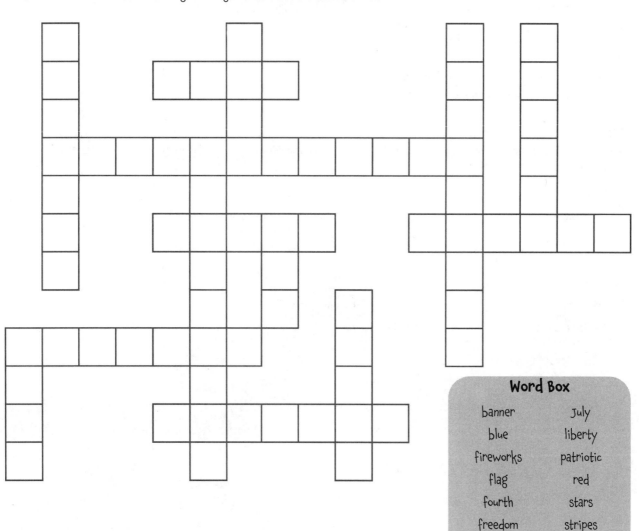

Word Box

banner	July
blue	liberty
fireworks	patriotic
flag	red
fourth	stars
freedom	stripes
independence	white

216 • Independence Day

What Makes a Nation Great?

I will walk in freedom, for I have devoted myself to [God's] commandments. **Psalm 119:45**

What You Need
- Crayons or markers

Preparation
Photocopy this page, making one for each child.

What It's All About
The Fourth of July celebrates America's independence from England. As Christians, our freedom from sin is something to celebrate every day.

What To Do
To fill in the blanks in the verse below, locate the letters on the United States flag. The first number under each blank refers to the number beside a stripe. The second number refers to the letter's place in the row, starting from the left. The letter for the first blank is G (4 = fourth stripe. 4 = fourth letter from the left.). When you complete the code, color the picture.

Row	Letters
1	S D R S A
2	E O T H E
3	I I S I U
4	T L A G N
5	X S N G E
6	E C S S y

__ __ __ __ __ __ __ __ __ **makes**
4-4 2-2 1-2 4-2 3-1 5-3 2-1 6-3 1-1

__ __ __ __ __ __ __ **great, but**
1-5 5-3 4-3 2-3 3-2 2-2 5-3

__ __ __ __ __ __
1-1 3-1 5-3 3-2 6-3 4-3

__ __ __ __ __ __ __
1-2 3-4 6-3 4-4 1-3 1-5 6-2 5-5

__ __ __ __ __ **people.**
4-1 2-2 1-5 5-3 6-5

Proverbs 14:34

My Fourth of July Day

Don't use your freedom to satisfy your sinful nature. Instead, use your freedom to serve one another in love. **Galatians 5:13**

What You Need
- Crayons or markers

Preparation
Photocopy this page, making one for each child.

What It's All About
The Fourth of July celebrates America's independence from England. As Christians, our freedom from sin is something to celebrate every day. Will you do your part to show honor and respect to your country, to your flag, and to God?

What To Do
Draw or write some things you could do to honor your country and God.

Happy Birthday, America

Godliness makes a nation great, but sin is a disgrace to any people. **Proverbs 14:34**

What It's All About

Independence Day is when we celebrate the birthday of our nation. We remember the heroic soldiers who fought to make us "one nation under God."

Color the picture below as a reminder that we too can look to God for guidance in our lives.

The Truth Will Set You Free

You will know the truth, and the truth will set you free. **John 8:32**

What It's All About

Because of a brave group of people who were not afraid of Britain's powerful army, the United States is a free and independent country today. What freedoms do we enjoy today?

Draw a freedom in the flag for which you can thank God (for example: church, school, prayer, etc.), and then color the rest of the picture.

Park Picnic

If my people who are called by my name will humble themselves and pray and seek my face and turn from their wicked ways, I will hear from heaven and will forgive their sins and restore their land. **2 Chronicles 7:14**

What It's All About

Have you ever read the inscription on a coin: "In God we trust"? Many of our nation's leaders truly trusted God and followed his Word. As you celebrate Independence Day with picnics, fireworks, and fun, remember that our ultimate source of freedom is found in Christ.

Draw picnic foods in the basket and a design on the kite, and then color the rest of the picture.

A Mind at Work

Commit your actions to the LORD, and your plans will succeed. **Proverbs 16:3**

What You Need

- Bibles • Pictures or actual replicas of tools and other instruments used by workers in the Bible

What It's All About

In 1894, Labor Day became an official holiday to celebrate workers. Many people get Labor Day Monday off from work so they can spend the long weekend with their families and friends. In Bible times, many workers did not have the luxury of taking the day off.

Craftsmen like carpenters, boat builders, weavers, and potters often passed their skills on to their children so they could help the family make a living. The Bible tells us that Jesus grew up helping his father Joseph with his carpentry trade (Matthew 13:55). Today, we're going to look at some tools from Bible times.

What To Do

Show the picture of each tool named in the table below. Children guess who in the Bible used the item and what their occupation might have been. If no one guesses correctly, read the Scripture reference. The first to correctly guess the answer recites, or choses a volunteer to recite, the memory verse.

Tool	Used By	Scripture
Shepherd's Crook	David (shepherd)	1 Samuel 17:15
Saw or Hammer	Joseph or Jesus (carpenter)	Matthew 13:55
Fishing Nets	Peter, Andrew, James, or John (fisherman)	Matthew 4:18–21
Coins or Abacus	Matthew or Zacchaeus (tax collector)	Matthew 9:9, Luke 19:2
Sword	centurion (army officer)	Luke 7:2–3,8
Small Tent	Paul (tent maker)	Acts 18:3
Purple Cloth	Lydia (purple cloth seller)	Acts 16:14
Needle and Thread	Dorcas (seamstress)	Acts 9:39
Medicine	Luke (doctor)	Colossians 4:14
Scroll	John (writer)	Revelation 1:4
Whisk or Cooking Pots	Martha (cook)	Luke 10:40
Harp or Lyre	David	1 Samuel 16:22–23

Willing Worker Maze

Work willingly at whatever you do, as though you were working for the Lord rather than for people. **Colossians 3:23**

What You Need
- Crayons or markers

Preparation
Photocopy this page, making one for each child.

What It's All About
Labor Day is a special day to celebrate American workers. Without their hard work, we wouldn't have the country that we have today. Working can be fun if you're doing an interesting task. But have you ever been given a chore that you really didn't want to do? It's hard to have a good attitude about work when your chores are not fun. The Bible tells us that when we work, we should do it as if we are working for God. The next time you are given a boring or difficult task, remember Colossians 3:23 and keep your mindset on God.

What to Do
Follow the words of Colossians 3:23 to complete the maze. Then write the verse words on the lines below.

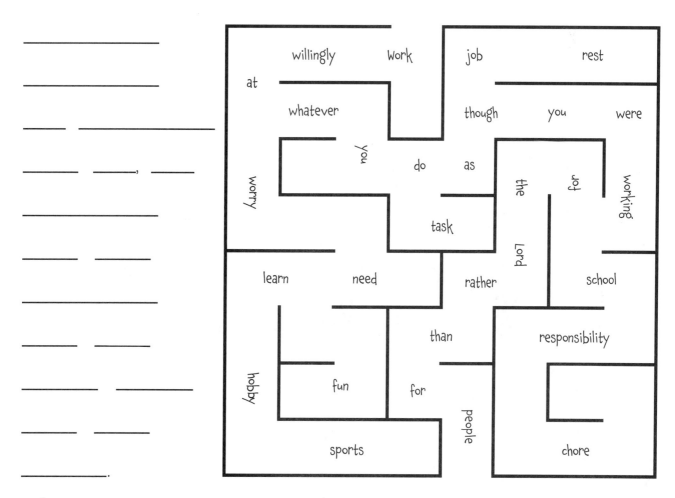

Colossians 3:23

Honor the Sabbath Day

Remember to observe the Sabbath day by keeping it holy. You have six days each week for your ordinary work, but the seventh day is a Sabbath day of rest dedicated to the LORD your God. **Exodus 20:8–10**

What It's All About

Once a year, Americans celebrate Labor Day by taking time off from work to spend with family or friends. Jewish people celebrate the day of rest, the *Sabbath* or *Shabbat*, once a week. It starts on Friday at sunset and ends on Saturday at sunset. This special day reminds Jewish people that God created the world in six days and on the seventh day, he rested. Jesus would have grown up celebrating the sabbath with his family.

Add fruits like grapes and figs to the dishes on the table. Color the picture of Jesus and his disciples sharing a sabbath meal.

Grandparents Day Celebration

I will be your God throughout your lifetime—until your hair is white with age. **Isaiah 46:4**

What It's All About

The Bible is filled with examples of older believers encouraging and guiding younger believers. Paul thanked God for Timothy's faith which lived in his grandmother, his mother, and also in him (2 Timothy 1:5). Grandparents deserve respect and honor because they are valuable members of God's household of faith. If your grandparents or other older family members are Christians, you can ask them for advice to live a godly life. As you get older, you'll appreciate the wisdom an older generation can offer.

Send Invitations

Two weeks before Grandparents Day, children make and send invitations to their grandparents to visit their class on Grandparents Day. Arrange for children who do not have grandparents living nearby to adopt an older person in the congregation for the day. Urge the "grandparents" to participate in every activity in the class along with the children.

Write Love Notes

The week before the grandparents visit, have children write special "love" messages to each visitor. Help the children hide the love messages around the classroom before their grandparents arrive on their special day. As part of the festivities, the guests search the room (with the help of the children) to find their messages.

Serve the Grandparents

Encourage children to serve the grandparents at snack time, offer them a chair, and in other ways act as their host throughout the class session.

Interview a Grandparent

What You Need

- Interview a Grandparent (p. 226) • Crayons or markers

Preparation

Photocopy Interview a Grandparent, making one or more for every grandparent.

What to Do

Children ask grandparents questions about their life. Shake things up by having kids interview a grandparent other than their own! Make sure each grandparent gets interviewed.

Interview a Grandparent

Teach us to realize the brevity of life, so that we may grow in wisdom. **Psalm 90:12**

What To Do

Ask a grandparent the questions below and write down their answers. Then, draw a picture of them in the space provided.

1. What is your full name?
   _____

2. Where were you born?
   _____

3. What was your favorite food as a kid?
   _____

4. What is the best thing about where you grew up?
   _____

5. What was your favorite toy or game when you were my age?
   _____
   _____

6. Did you have any pets when you were my age? What kind?
   _____
   _____

7. What was your favorite subject in school? Why?
   _____
   _____

8. What do you remember about the day we met?
   _____
   _____

9. How old were you when you became a Christian? Where did it happen?
   _____
   _____

10. What is your favorite Bible verse?
    _____
    _____

Our Best Memories

Gray hair is a crown of glory; it is gained by living a godly life. **Proverbs 16:31**

What To Do

Draw pictures of your favorite memories with your grandparents, older family members, or guardians. Then, write a short description for each picture. Give it to them on Grandparents Day to show them how much you care.

1. _____
   _____
   _____
   _____
   _____
   _____
   _____

2. _____
   _____
   _____
   _____
   _____
   _____
   _____

3. _____
   _____
   _____
   _____
   _____
   _____
   _____

Grandparents Day

Happy Grandparents Day

Grandchildren are the crowning glory of the aged; parents are the pride of their children. **Proverbs 17:6**

What It's All About

Grandparents, older family members, or guardians are awesome for snuggles, snacks, and so much more! What are some of your favorite things to do with your them?

Write a note on the back of this coloring page describing your favorite things to do together. Then, color the picture and send it to them.

We Love with Our Actions

Dear children, let's not merely say that we love each other; let us show the truth by our actions. **1 John 3:18**

What It's All About

Because God showed his love for us through Jesus, we should show our love for others. The Bible says that it is not good enough to merely tell people that we love them. We must show them our love by our actions and how we treat them. Our actions really do speak louder than words. How is the boy in this picture showing his love for his grandmother?

Color the picture and draw the colorful leaves that the boy is raking.

Grandparents Day • 229

© 2021 Rose Publishing, LLC. Permission to photocopy granted to original purchaser only. *The Super-Sized Book of Holidays, Special Days, & Celebrations.*

Texture Ship

Be strong and courageous! Do not be afraid or discouraged. For the LORD *your God is with you wherever you go.* **Joshua 1:9**

What You Need
- Texture Ship Sheet (p. 231) • Card stock
- Crayons or markers • Cotton balls
- Glue • Ribbons • Scissors
- Blue construction paper
- Fish-shaped crackers

Preparation
Photocopy Texture Ship Sheet on card stock, making one for each child.

What It's All About
Columbus Day celebrates Christopher Columbus's arrival in North America. Columbus was a European explorer who sailed with three ships: the *Niña*, the *Pinta*, and the *Santa Maria*. Before Columbus started his journey, he had a hard time raising funds for the supplies to cross the Atlantic Ocean. We often face challenges when striving toward a goal.

When you face a challenge, pray and ask God for help. He will help you along the way. He will provide the means, clear the way, and give the strength you need to accomplish the task. Today, we'll decorate a ship like Columbus's as a reminder that God is with you wherever you go.

What To Do
1. Color the Texture Ship Sheet.
2. Gently stretch the cotton balls.
3. Glue cotton balls in the sky for clouds.
4. Cut and glue ribbons for the flags.
5. Cut out waves from blue construction paper and glue them under the ship.
6. Glue fish-shaped crackers on the water.

Texture Ship Sheet

"God is with you wherever you go."
Joshua 1:9

Columbus Day • 231

© 2021 Rose Publishing, LLC. Permission to photocopy granted to original purchaser only. *The Super-Sized Book of Holidays, Special Days, & Celebrations.*

Hands Down the Best Pastor

All Scripture is inspired by God and is useful to teach us what is true. **2 Timothy 3:16**

What You Need

- Poster board • Markers • Colored construction paper • Scissors • Glue

Preparation

In the center of the poster board, write "You are hands down the best pastor!" Also include the class's grade, name of Sunday School class (if you have one), "Pastor Appreciation Day," and the year. Be sure that there is enough space around the edges to glue on the children's hands. It's OK if the hands extend past the edge.

Optional: Feel free to get creative with the shape of the poster board. You can cut it into a big heart or star.

If you have a large class, you may need multiple poster boards.

What It's All About

Pastor Appreciation Day is a special day to honor our church leaders by recognizing all their hard work. Today, we'll get to honor them with this hands-on craft.

What to Do

1. Trace one hand on colored construction paper.
2. Cut out the hand.
3. On your paper hand, write a thank you note for your pastor. Get creative! On each finger you could write a word that describes them and then write your thank you on the palm. You can even draw a picture on the palm. Don't forget to add your name at the bottom of the hand.
4. Glue the hand to the edge of the poster board.

Bonus Idea

While your pastor is preaching the sermon, decorate their office with your posters.

Pastor Crossword

Those who are the greatest among you should take the lowest rank, and the leader should be like a servant. **Luke 22:26**

What You Need
- Crayons or markers

Preparation
Photocopy this page, making one for each child.

What It's All About
A PASTOR is a LEADER of a CHURCH, and they can have many different roles. They READ the BIBLE throughout the week to prepare for their SERMON. They PREACH about FAITH in God and MENTOR believers. Some might visit the sick and LISTEN to their PRAYERs because they CARE. What is something that you can do to show your pastor that you appreciate all their hard work? Write your answers below.

_____

_____

_____

_____

What to Do
Fill in the crossword with the capitalized words above. A few letters have been filled in for you. Hint: Count the letters in each word. Then, begin by filling in the shortest words first. Color the picture.

Pastor Appreciation Day

Corny Craft

Grow in the grace and knowledge of our Lord and Savior Jesus Christ. **2 Peter 3:18**

What You Need

- Corn Patterns (p. 235) • White card stock • Scissors • Green and yellow construction paper
- Glue • Green, yellow, and black markers • Unpopped popcorn kernels

Preparation

Photocopy Corn Patterns on white card stock, making one for every three children.

What It's All About

When you plant a garden, you carefully till the soil, make straight narrow rows, drop the seeds down into the soil, and then cover them up. What do you expect to happen next? You expect your garden to grow!

You might have a very good start, but if you want your garden to grow, you have to take a few more steps. You must make sure your garden gets enough water and sunshine. When little green shoots appear, you have to pull the weeds out so that the plants do not choke. Then, if there are a lot of birds or animals around, you may have to put up a scarecrow or build a fence around your garden.

Our lives are like planted fields or gardens. We might have a good start when we become Christians, but growing in God requires a few more steps. We must read God's Word and pray to get our roots grounded. We need to go to church and learn God's Word. We need to surround ourselves with Christian friends to help guard against temptation. When we do these things, our lives will blossom and we will be fruitful.

What To Do

1. Trace and cut one set of leaves from green construction paper.
2. Trace and cut one ear of corn from yellow paper.
3. Glue corn on a sheet of white card stock.
4. Glue the leaves over the corn as shown in the finished product image.
5. Outline the leaves with a green marker and the corn with yellow.
6. With a black marker, write the memory verse on the green leaves.
7. Starting at the bottom of the corn cob, carefully glue unpopped popcorn kernels in tight rows all the way up the cob.

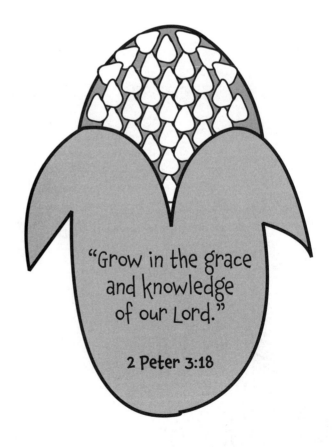

Corn Patterns

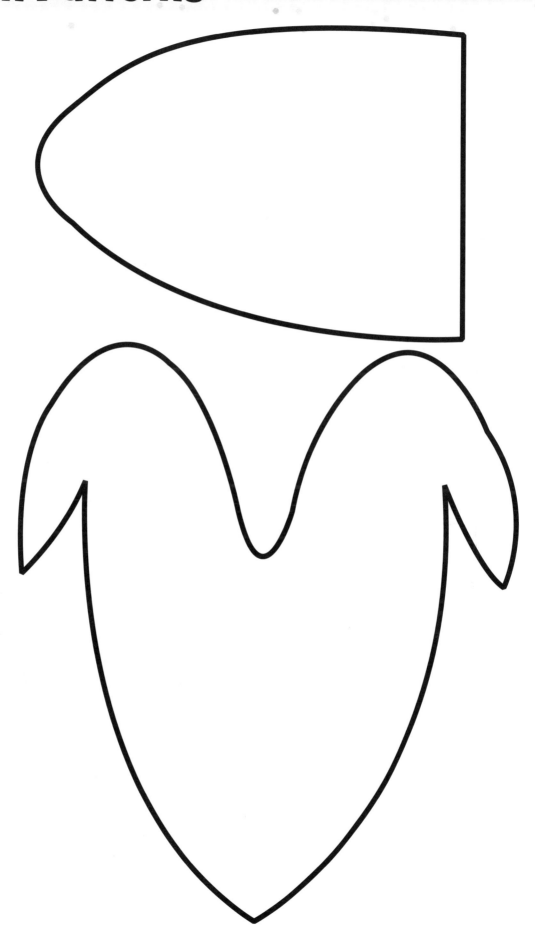

Crayon Leaf Placemats

God has made everything beautiful. **Ecclesiastes 3:11**

What You Need

- Leaf Patterns (p. 237) • White card stock • Waxed paper
- Old red, yellow, and orange crayons • Pencil sharpeners • Old towel • Iron (for adult use only) • Scissors
- 12x18-inch yellow construction paper • Glue • Permanent black marker • Clear Con-Tact paper

Preparation

Photocopy Leaf Patterns on card stock, making one for each child. Tear off pieces of waxed paper, making one for each child. Waxed-paper pieces should be about the size of a place mat. Spread old towel on a table away from where children will be working. Plug in an iron nearby, but out of the reach of children. This will be the ironing station, for adult use only.

What It's All About

Autumn is traditionally a time to celebrate the harvest. It is a beautiful time of year, especially in places where the leaves turn to colors of red, yellow, and orange. God has created many beautiful things for which we can be thankful.

What are some other things that he made that are beautiful? We know that God exists because of all we see around us. The Bible says that God created everything. How fortunate we are to live in this beautiful world God made! Let's make colorful placemats that we can use to celebrate the season!

What To Do

1. Lay out a piece of waxed-paper to work on.
2. Peel the paper from three or four different colors of crayons.
3. Use the pencil sharpeners to shave the crayons, letting the shavings fall onto the waxed paper.
4. When you have a nice variety of shavings, push them to one half of the waxed paper.
5. Distribute shavings evenly, staying away from the edges. Then fold the other side of the waxed paper over them.
6. Carefully take the paper to the adult at the ironing station for ironing on the old towel. See Ironing Station sidebar.
7. After the paper cools slightly, adult hands paper back to the child. Child then cuts out the leaf pattern and traces two on the waxed paper, then cut them out.
8. Arrange the leaves on a sheet of yellow construction paper and glue them down, leaving room to write the memory verse.
9. With a black marker, write the memory verse.
10. Cover placemats with clear Con-Tact paper.

Ironing Station

Cover the paper with an old towel and gently iron the paper on a low setting until the colors run together and the waxed paper seals. Do not allow children to use the iron and do not leave the iron unattended. If you have a large class, consider asking another adult to assist you.

Leaf Patterns

Sweet Treats

How sweet your words taste to me; they are sweeter than honey. **Psalm 119:103**

What It's All About

Over many centuries, Halloween became a day of costumes, candy, and festive parties. In Bible times, if they wanted to eat something sweet, they ate fruits or honey. It's always exciting to receive Halloween candy. Which is your favorite?

What to Do

Figure out the candy clues below and write the answers on the blanks. The circles in the middle will give you some advice on how to best enjoy your candy. Then, color the candy.

1. Peanut butter and chocolate
2. Makers of a kiss of chocolate
3. Colorful chewy candy "exploding" with flavor
4. Another name for a happy farmer
5. Looks like red rope
6. Crispy chocolate-covered wafer bar
7. Sounds like a famous baseball player (or a very young girl's name)
8. If you chew, it could break your jaw
9. Name of our galaxy
10. Small round colorful candies
11. Chewy red sea creature

1. _ _ _ _ _ _ ' _   Pieces
2. _ _ _ _ _ _ _
3. _ _ _ _ _ _ _ _ _ _ _ _
4. _ _ _ _ _ _ _ _ _
5. _ _ _ _ _ _ _ _ _
6. _ _ _ _ _ _ _
7. _ _ _ _ _ _ _ _
8. _ _ _ _ _ _ _ _ _
9. _ _ _ _ _ _ _ _
10. _ _ _ _ _ _ _
11. _ _ _ _ _ _ _ _ _ _ _

Sweet Treats: (1) Reese's Pieces (2) Hershey (3) Starburst (4) Jolly Rancher (5) Twizzlers (6) Kit Kat (7) Babe Ruth (8) Jawbreaker (9) Milky Way (10) Skittles (11) Swedish Fish (Circle answer) Share Treats.

Happy Pumpkin Word Search

*You light a lamp for me. The L*ORD*, my God, lights up my darkness.* **Psalm 18:28**

What It's All About

Pumpkins begin as tiny seeds but grow into big orange vegetables. They can be carved into smiley faces, hearts, and messages of hope. When a candle is put inside the pumpkin, these designs glow. In the same way, when you are filled with the Holy Spirit and the hope of the gospel, you smile. Find the happy harvest words in the word search below. Remember to spread God's love wherever you go.

Word Box

abundant	pumpkin
apples	reap
autumn	ripe
crop	sickle
fall	sow
grain	wheat
plant	

```
            N N C
          U A F M C S A W D
        S B L G D P T T I B I Q U
      G P W W B Z N N H Q E V U S V R S
      Z K K W J J E Z S E R P L Y N A U P H
    Q B B I M L L P U M P K I N A X D Q L W J
    G J W Z Z E T Q P P E J F T O P B A A A C
    O K Q V R O     V K B P J     P L N G L U
    U W B V M M     H Z N Y B     I L T T L K
    Q J H B Q D S I C K L E A C L P S V T P E E C E T
    A Y E H Y L O H R S S O I Z M C M O C A R S Z X H
    K T A Y K B E N P N V P J G S N K T W F D V N Q B
    P E R T X H E R Z M D W K D U T D S T H J H O M B O Y
    I L J D P Y O Q X A D T V F B V E B P C E R X B M L U
    G R W M G C D P O N A Y H X R V I V I R E H F H C N J
    L C M L   P Z I P Y E K B R T O D J O R   W O J N
    N G W O     A U T U M N A R W A C Y P     T Z Z C
    V E R H R     V U E T H E M Z H C L     I D W L E
      X F A R R                           N L A H O
      J X C I F D                         R D O V M J
        K I P N A F T B D R D Y Y E Q D Z K K Y R
        H Z E R P L K S A V U J I N L W T U L U Z
          W P L Q T L R O S I F S E X O V Y I X
            V Y Q M M E S S C E T O D Q U N S
              V D T A M Q L X Q A I R V
                F P B D W R S E V
                    M E I
```

Halloween Alternatives

Noah's Ark Celebration

God made all sorts of wild animals, livestock, and small animals, each able to produce offspring of the same kind. And God saw that it was good. **Genesis 1:25**

Animal Ark Invites

Turn Halloween into something positive with a Bible-centered animal-themed Noah's Ark celebration! Send out invitations that look like boat tickets or animal passports. Invite children dress as animals and to bring friends. Give a special prize to those who come as matching pairs.

Read Animal Stories from the Bible

- Share animal-themed Bible stories. Some examples besides Noah's Ark are Moses's snake on a pole, Daniel in the lion's den, Balaam's talking donkey, or Jonah and the big fish.
- For over 200 animal-themed activities and stories checkout RoseKidz's *Top 50 Bible Lessons with God's Amazing Animals* at www.hendricksonrose.com/rosekidz

Circus Snacks

Provide animal-themed snacks like animal crackers, fish-shaped crackers, or fruit roll ups (label them as frog tongues). For extra fun, label the drinks with cute critter names like Ladybug Liquid, Tree Frog Tonic, Jellyfish Juice, or Rainforest Refreshments.

Three-Legged Race

The animals entered Noah's Ark in pairs. Pair up children of similar height and tie one player's left foot to the other player's right foot. Players line up at a start line and must race to the finish without falling. The first to the finish must reference a Bible animal story other than Noah's Ark.

Paper Boat Race

Search online for instructions for creating paper boats. Children line up their boats at one end of the table and fan or blow them to the other side. The first child to get their boat across recites, or chooses someone to recite, the memory verse.

Crazy Animal Card Game

What You Need

- Animals Cards (pp. 241–242) • Scissors or paper cutter

Preparation

Photocopy Animal Cards, making one copy for every four children. Cut out the cards. Optional: Laminating cards or covering them with clear Con-Tact paper or packing tape will make them more durable.

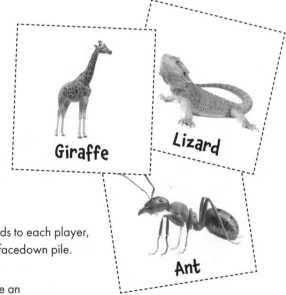

What To Do

1. Form groups of four with one deck of Animals Cards for each group.
2. Play a game like Crazy Eights. The dealer for each group deals five cards to each player, turns the first card up on the table, and places the remaining cards in a facedown pile.
3. The player to the left of the dealer looks at their hand for a card with a similarity to the card facing up: for example, a zebra. This would include an animal that has four legs, stripes, a mane, starts with the letter Z, etc.
   - If the child finds a match, they place it on top of the zebra card and say the connection aloud: "My tiger has stripes like a zebra."
   - If the child does not have any animal cards with any zebra similarities, they pick up a card from the deck.
4. Play moves to the next child. Continue until one child has no cards left, or as time allows.

Light-of-the-World Celebration

[Jesus] said, "I am the light of the world. If you follow me, you won't have to walk in darkness, because you will have the light that leads to life. **John 8:12**

Optional Preparation

Dim the lights and hand out glow sticks, glow necklaces, or flashlights. Arrange flameless votives or tealights around the room.

What It's All About

Halloween, or "All Hallows Eve," first began as a Celtic holiday celebrated on October 31 where people would light bonfires to scare off evil spirits. In the eighth century, Pope Gregory III made November 1 a special day to honor saints, and the church used All Hallows Eve to prepare for the new holiday. Saints are Christians who lived lives that honored God. Many of them even died for their faith.

Today, we can celebrate Jesus' victory over death, sin, and darkness. He is the light of the world. There is nothing more powerful than God's gospel message of love. Let's celebrate!

> **Optional: Letters to Missionaries**
>
> Organize a table showcasing pictures of the missionaries supported by your church. Provide paper and pens for people to write notes or draw pictures to thank them for bringing the light of Jesus to the world.

Light-of-the-World Torch Craft

What You Need

- Bible • Scissors • Red, orange, and yellow tissue paper • Colored construction paper
- Paper-towel tube, one for each child • Glue • Markers • Children's worship music and player

Preparation

- Cut yellow tissue paper into approximately 12x12-inch squares, making one for each child.
- Cut orange tissue paper into approximately 10x10-inch squares, making one for each child.
- Cut red tissue paper into approximately 9x9-inch squares, making one for each child.

What To Do

1. Apply glue to a piece of colored construction paper and wrap it around the paper-towel tube. Cut off any excess paper.
2. Look up one of the following verses: Psalm 23:4, Psalm 27:1, Psalm 119:105, John 8:12, or 2 Timothy 1:7. Write your favorite on your tube.
3. Layer the tissue paper on top of each other with the yellow at the bottom, the orange in the middle, and the red on top.
4. Pinch the center of the tissue paper and pull up. Continue to pinch and twist the end of the tissue paper until you have a little handle. This is your flame.
5. Apply glue to the top of the paper-towel tube.
6. Push the tissue-paper handle inside the tube. Hold for a minute until the glue dries.
7. Sing worship songs as you march around the room holding your flames high in a light parade.

> For another light-themed craft turn to Cross Sun Catchers on page 44.

Read True Stories with Flashlights

- Search online for short stories about Christian saints or devout believers. Some examples include Amy Carmichael, St. Augustine, Mother Theresa, Corrie ten Boom, or Dietrich Bonhoeffer. Read the stories to the children.
- Read The Way of the Cross on page 43.
- After you've read the story, remind children that Jesus is the light of the world and his power overcomes everything.

Sing Songs about Victory over Death

Search for Christian songs with themes of God's light overcoming darkness, death, and the grave.

Missionary Mission

Don't use your freedom to satisfy your sinful nature. Instead, use your freedom to serve one another in love. **Galatians 5:13**

What It's All About

A missionary is a believer sent to share the news that Jesus died for our sins. Missionaries make incredible sacrifices like leaving their families, friends, and homes so that they can serve God. You can support a missionary in many ways. Writing letters is one method. Sending money is another way to help, but keeping them in your prayers is the most important.

Write a prayer for a missionary below. Keep this sheet at your bedside to remind you to pray for missionaries every night.

Children's Talent Show

So, my children, listen to me, for all who follow my ways are joyful. **Proverbs 8:32**

What You Need
- Crayons or markers

Preparation
Photocopy this page, making one for each child.

What It's All About
Universal Children's Day is celebrated on November 20. It is a day to celebrate what makes children special. To Jesus, children are considered a gift from God. Jesus clearly expressed his love for children, and he commanded his disciples to do the same (Matthew 19:14).

Jesus looks at the things that are important, such as our attitudes, what we do with the talents and abilities he gave us, how we treat others, and how we treat him. God has given you many gifts and talents, and those are all things to celebrate.

What to Do
The week before Children's Day, explain that you are going to invite the entire congregation to see the things children can do. Ask children to bring samples of their hobbies to class the following week, in the form of songs, poems, artwork, etc. Help them compose a class litany or song about their being made in the image of God that can be presented for the guests. Children can also help prepare refreshments to serve guests.

On the blank lines below, children brainstorm about some ideas for the talent show. Then, color the picture of Jesus and the children, and post it in your room as a reminder to come prepared on Children's Day.

_____

_____

_____

_____

_____

_____

_____

_____

_____

_____

Let the Children Come

Jesus said, "Let the children come to me. Don't stop them! For the Kingdom of Heaven belongs to those who are like these children." **Matthew 19:14**

What It's All About

One day when Jesus was teaching crowds of people, parents brought their children for Jesus to bless. His disciples tried to keep them away because Jesus was busy talking to the adults. But Jesus didn't like that. He told the disciples to let the children come. He said that the kingdom of Heaven belongs to children like these. What did he mean by that? He meant that anyone who rushes to God with joy and great faith belongs in Heaven. Draw yourself to the left of Jesus. As you color the picture below, think of how you can be a child of God.

The Greatest Gift Ever Given

The generous will prosper; those who refresh others will themselves be refreshed. **Proverbs 11:25**

What It's All About

Boxing Day is celebrated every year on December 26. The holiday originated in the United Kingdom and is celebrated by many other countries that were once part of the British Empire. Originally, Boxing Day was a day off for servants to bring boxes of Christmas leftovers to their families. Today, it's celebrated by giving gifts or extra tips to service workers.

Many also donate food and clothing to the poor on this day. The greatest gift ever given was God's sacrifice for our sins. Will you share the greatest gift with others by being generous with your time, money, and kindness?

Draw a bow on the gift and color the picture. Think of someone who you'd share God's gift with and write their name on the tag.

Seven Principles Search

I appeal to you, dear brothers and sisters, by the authority of our Lord Jesus Christ, to live in harmony with each other. **1 Corinthians 1:10**

What It's All About

Kwanzaa is an African-American celebration held from December 26 to January 1. It honors the importance of family, community, and African-American culture. Each family celebrates a little differently, but many include songs, dances, storytelling, and a large meal. One important tradition is lighting the *KINARA*, a candle holder that holds seven candles—one black, three red, and three green. Families light one candle for each day of the celebration week and discuss one of the seven Kwanzaa principles: UNITY, SELF-DETERMINATION, COLLECTIVE WORK and RESPONSIBILITY, COOPERATIVE ECONOMICS, PURPOSE, CREATIVITY, and FAITH.

What to Do

In the word search, find the words in all caps from the story. Note that self-determination is hidden as two separate words. Then, color the pictures.

```
            C C A P                O H W W
          S R F O U A            Y C O E Q C
        S R E G I R Q C        E L O P I F X O
      Q Q T A S A I D E T E R M I N A T I O N
    X H L B T N Y R C R D M E Q F H Q F Y F H A
  K C C W O I V K N W O H U N J E F L J L U B L V
  Z J U N K V G C F R H O V I M W L F E M H Y K M
  X C N F A I T H G E K P P B P O W S W E Y D N R
  L U I J Y T H W G S G W F E D R A Q I I E S U A
  U R T I F Y W D F P H L I H R K M Q W V V D J K
  I W Y B E O Z A B O C L C X A A E K I S S Z C E
    G P P P J D O E N Q G B R N J T T C L U W H
    C Z J S U K L W S J Q G G K T C I F B I W U
          D H R U X O C I Q W L M E E M X V B O G
          W I Y O D W B H G B G L O C U U E O
            P Z V X F I L Y A L N M V L S D
            Q C T G L M W O O O S X O X
              Z G G I N C C J I W P L
                Y Q T G E L C W R V
                  J Y T K Z D U J
                    H C Q B P S
                      T S P L
                        R Q
```

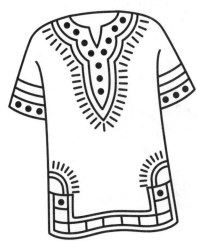

Birthday Thoughts

God keeps such people so busy enjoying life that they take no time to brood over the past. **Ecclesiastes 5:20**

What It's All About

God has given us so many things to make us happy. Growing up is one of them. We can thank God for giving us another year to do our best in serving him. Jesus had birthdays, too, to mark his growing years. Do you think that Jesus' family celebrated his birthday? How does your family celebrate your birthday?

Birthday Bear

So encourage each other and build each other up, just as you are already doing. **1 Thessalonians 5:11**

What You Need
- Birthday Ark (p. 251) • Crayons or markers

Preparation
Photocopy one or both birthday greeting sheets, making one for each child.

What It's All About
God asks us to encourage our fellow believers in their faith. We can do this by sharing Scripture, praying for others, and sharing what we have. Birthdays are great opportunities for encouraging others. Give the Birthday Ark page to someone who is having a birthday to encourage them in their faith.

On the Birthday Ark page, draw animals on the art next to Noah. Then color the picture and give it to someone who's having a birthday.

250 • Birthdays

© 2021 Rose Publishing, LLC. Permission to photocopy granted to original purchaser only. *The Super-Sized Book of Holidays, Special Days, & Celebrations.*

Birthday Ark

To: _____

From: _____

These animals on Noah's Ark
Have come along your way
To wish for you the very best
On this, your Happy Birthday!

Happy Birthday!

Graduation Caps

For everything there is a season, a time for every activity under heaven. **Ecclesiastes 3:1**

What You Need
- Scissors • Ruler • Poster board • Construction paper • Crayons or markers
- Decorative materials (stickers, glitter, sequins, etc.) • Stapler • Glue • Yarn • Thread • Tape

What It's All About
The last day of school is usually a mixture of sadness and excitement. It's exciting because you're moving up to a new grade with new teachers and new subjects. But it can be sad because you might miss the way things used to be. Our memory verse tells us that there is a time for everything. Make a graduation cap as a reminder that nothing stays the same forever.

What To Do
1. Cut a 10-inch poster-board square and a 3x20-inch construction-paper strip.
2. Decorate one side of your poster board square with crayons or markers and decorative elements.
3. Fold down one inch along the long edge of the strip and cut notches in the folded part.
4. Staple the strip into a circle and glue the notched edge to the poster-board square.
5. For a tassel, cut eleven 10-inch pieces of yarn.
6. Tie ten pieces of yarn at their center with the other 10-inch piece of yarn.
7. Fold the pieces of yarn in half and tie securely with a piece of thread or string a half inch below the center fold.
8. Tape the tassel to the brim of the cap.

Bonus
- Display children's achievements from the past year in Bible study, memory work, and attendance. Recognize the completion of special assignments or outstanding accomplishments.
- Consider presenting special certificates to the children to recognize their efforts.
- Arrange displays in the room that show the projects children have completed during the year. Invite parents and friends to visit the room with their child. Encourage children to be tour guides, explaining the various projects and displays.

> Younger children can make simple paper crowns as an alternative to graduation caps.

Vacation Books

I am with you, and I will protect you wherever you go. **Genesis 28:15**

What You Need

- Paper • 3 Hole punch • Binder, one for each child, or construction paper

What to Do

1. Make the books by typing or printing one entry suggestion on each page, allowing plenty of room for the child to write or draw. Make six to eight pages total. Photocopy enough pages for each child to have one. Possible entries are:

    I left on my trip at ___ o'clock, on _____ (day). I felt _____ . I traveled on a _____ (car, boat, airplane, train). Here is a picture of what I first saw.

    OR

    I began my vacation on _____ (day). I felt _____. Here is a picture of the first thing I did.
    The funniest thing that happened to me so far was _____ .
    This is a picture postcard of something I found interesting.
    Today we visited _____.
    We have some interesting souvenirs. I found or bought _____ .

2. Three-hole punch the pages and place them into colorful binders or staple a construction paper cover over them to make a vacation book for each child.

3. Include your own take-home papers for the Sundays that the child will be away.

4. On the Sunday before summer vacation, present the books to the children.

> Vacation books can become an effective bridge between vacationing children and the Sunday school. Even shy children are usually ready to share unique experiences of a trip or a vacation.

Suggested Reproducibles to Include for Summer

- We Are Abraham's Family (p. 206)
- Celebration Crossword (p. 216)
- What Makes a Nation Great? (p. 217)
- My Fourth of July Day (p. 218)
- Happy Birthday America (p. 219)
- Park Picnic (p. 221)
- Let the Children Come (p. 246)

> If a child has a summer birthday, consider adding one of the birthday coloring pages (pp. 249–251). For easy distribution, put a sticky note on the binders that include summer birthday pages.

Bonus

Reserve one Sunday early in the fall for a travel-themed party. Feature interviews, displays, and the completed vacation books. Lead into a time of expressing praise and appreciation to God for the opportunities for seeing his creation and for his loving care and protection while traveling.

For those children who will be staying home during vacation, provide a similar book for them to keep track of interesting things they have done at home. No one should be left out of the fun of sharing their summer vacation.

Top 50 Teaching Resources

The Top 50 series aims to provide the top resources for children's ministries. Enjoy the quick and easy-to-use reproducible resources packed with lessons, activities, and crafts. Includes top lessons every child should know that are volunteer- and child-friendly.

256+ pages each, Paperback, Black & White

Top 50 Instant Bible Lessons for Preschoolers	R50002	ISBN: 9781628624977
Top 50 Instant Bible Lessons for Elementary	R50003	ISBN: 9781628624984
Top 50 Memory Verse Lessons	R50010	ISBN: 9781628625059
Top 50 Bible Object Lessons	R50009	ISBN: 9781628625042
Top 50 Creative Bible Lessons	R38255	ISBN: 9781584111566
Top 50 Science-Based Bible Lessons	R50022	ISBN: 9781628629606
Top 50 Bible Lessons with God's Amazing Animals	R50023	ISBN: 9781628629637
Top 50 Bible Stories about Jesus for Preschool	R50014	ISBN: 9781628629736
Top 50 Bible Stories about Jesus for Elementary	R50026	ISBN: 9781628629743

Find more great books by visiting **www.hendricksonrose.com/RoseKidz.**

Take Your Kids on a Journey from Creation to Revelation!

The Bible spans thousands of years. How can you help kids get the big picture? Exploring the Bible through History is the ONLY teaching resource that features Bible curriculum as part of a visual time line. Show kids ages 5–10 when these 25 key Bible stories really happened!

Enjoy These Key Features:

24 full-color Bible lessons, plus a bonus lesson

125 flexible activities and over **300** discussion questions

24 reproducible coloring pages (Also available as a PDF download!)

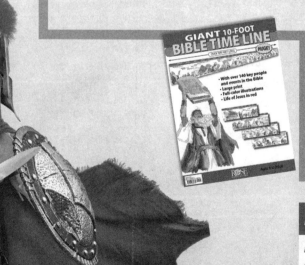

Plus! Each lesson includes interactive options to use with Rose's best-selling Giant 10-Foot Bible Time Line.

Get It Today!

Exploring the Bible through History	$19.99	ISBN: 9781628627855
Exploring the Bible through History Coloring Time Line (PDF Download)	$12.99	ISBN: 9781649380241
Giant 10-Foot Bible Time Line	$19.99	ISBN: 9781596360679

www.hendricksonrose.com/rosekidz